The Sixteenth-Century Hero

Rightly Dividing the Word of Truth

———•◆•———

Under the series title Rightly Dividing the Word of Truth, the Reformed Free Publishing Association (RFPA) continues publication of its paperback series. Based on solidly Reformed biblical exegesis and lively application of the Reformed creeds, the chapters of these volumes originally appeared as articles in the *Standard Bearer*, the semi-monthly periodical also published by the RFPA. The goal of publishing this series is to give broader life to the subjects as originally treated by the *Standard Bearer* editorial staff. The RFPA intends to continue this series on a variety of timely topics.

Books in this series include:

David. J. Engelsma, *Common Grace Revisited*
David J. Engelsma, Barry Gritters, Charles Terpstra, *Reformed Worship*
David J. Engelsma, editor, *The Sixteenth-Century Reformation of the Church*

Additional titles are under consideration.

The Sixteenth-Century Reformation of the Church

Edited by
David J. Engelsma

Reformed Free Publishing Association
Jenison, Michigan

© 2007 Reformed Free Publishing Association
All rights reserved
Printed in the United States of America

No part of this book may be used or reprinted in any form without permission from the publisher, except in the case of a brief quotation used in connection with a critical article or review. Material of this book was originally published in special Reformation issues of the *Standard Bearer*, October 1990–October 2003.

Scriptures cited are taken from the
Authorized (King James) Version of the Bible

For information, contact:
Reformed Free Publishing Association
1894 Georgetown Center Dr.
Jenison, MI 49428-7137
Phone: (616) 457-5970
Fax: (616) 457-5980
Website: www.rfpa.org
E-mail: mail@rfpa.org

ISBN: 978-0-916206-95-6
LCCN: 2007922834

Contents

Preface   vii

Part 1: Lives

1. Martin Luther: Reformer and Defender of Truth,
   Garrett Eriks   3

2. John Calvin: Pastor and Teacher,
   Barry Gritters   10

3. Luther's Only Truly Congenial Disciple,
   David J. Engelsma   18

4. John Knox: Reformer and Preacher,
   Dale Kuiper   24

5. Calvin and Knox's Relationship of Mutual
   Love and Esteem, *David Higgs*   32

Part 2: History

6. The Reform of Geneva,
   Steven Key   41

7. God's Continuing Controversy with Unchanged
   Rome, *David J. Engelsma*   48

8. The History of Anabaptism,
   Herman Hanko   54

9. The Enemy on the Left,
   David J. Engelsma   60

Part 3: Doctrines and Issues

10 The Bible, a Divine Book: John Calvin's Doctrine of Holy Scripture,
   Dale Kuiper ... 69

11 The Reformation and Biblical Interpretation,
   Herman Hanko ... 75

12 "Far Brighter Even Than the Sun",
   David J. Engelsma ... 82

13 Luther on Preaching,
   Steven Key ... 88

14 Luther, Erasmus, and the Bondage of the Will,
   Russell Dykstra ... 96

15 Luther on Justification,
   Ronald Hanko ... 107

16 Calvin on Justification,
   Mark Shand ... 120

17 Rome's Dreadful Doctrine of Purgatory,
   Kenneth Koole ... 127

18 Piety and the Reformation, or the Reformation's Awed Love of God, David J. Engelsma ... 132

19 Calvin's Doctrine of the Christian Life,
   David J. Engelsma ... 139

20 Calvin's Liturgy,
   Robert Decker ... 149

21 Worship the Lord in Psalms,
   Herman Hanko ... 153

22 Calvin's Doctrine of Predestination, or Magnifying God's Grace by Double Predestination,
   Charles Terpstra ... 160

23 An Eschatology of Grace,
   David J. Engelsma ... 166

Endnotes ... 173

Contributors ... 193

Preface

Over the past nearly twenty years, it has been the editorial policy of the Reformed periodical, the *Standard Bearer*, to devote the October 15 issue, annually, to a commemoration of the sixteenth-century Reformation of the church. The writers, mostly ministers in the Protestant Reformed Churches in America, devoted all the articles in a particular issue to a certain aspect of the Reformation. Some issues treated the reformers themselves. Others dealt with the history. Still others examined certain important doctrines and various controversies.

From these special, Reformation issues of the *Standard Bearer*, the Reformed Free Publishing Association (RFPA) has selected the articles that are the content of this book. The articles are divided roughly into three groupings: biographical, historical, and doctrinal.

Although we have attempted to weave the articles more closely together by editing (which in no case affected the content of any article), it is plain that this book is no thorough, systematic treatment of the Reformation, or of any aspect of the Reformation.

Nevertheless, the book has its appeal and profit. The chapters are concise treatments of a reformer, a doctrine, a controversy, or an aspect of the history of the Reformation. The authors write for the people, not for the scholars. All the writers love the gospel recovered by the Reformation, honor that mighty movement as the work of Jesus Christ, and desire that all readers share this love and honor with them.

The discerning reader may even detect a line running through the book, made up though it is of disparate articles by different writers: the sovereignty of grace in the salvation of the elect church—*the* truth for which the Reformation contended.

The RFPA intends to publish a successor-volume in the "Rightly Dividing the Word of Truth" series. This volume will trace the Reformation to modern times.

—Prof. David J. Engelsma
Theological School of the
Protestant Reformed Churches

Part 1

Lives

1

Martin Luther: Reformer and Defender of Truth

Garrett Eriks

MARTIN LUTHER WAS BORN NOVEMBER 10, 1483 IN Eisleben in Prussian Saxony. His parents were very poor, but they were hard-working and pious members of the Roman Catholic Church. In home and in school, Luther was taught to be a good Roman Catholic. His parents taught Luther to pray to God and the saints, to revere the church, and to fear devils and witches. In school Luther learned the Lord's Prayer, the Ten Commandments, and several Latin and German hymns.

In 1501, at the age of eighteen, Luther entered the University of Erfurt, where he studied scholastic philosophy. Luther studied some of the ancient classics, and he sufficiently mastered Latin so that he could write it clearly. During these years of his education, Luther became concerned about his personal salvation. He often despaired because of his sinfulness and therefore was drawn to the study of theology. But according to the wish of his father, Luther began to study law.

Luther Becomes a Monk

God led Luther to the monastic life through two events.

First, the news of the sudden death of a friend shocked him. Second, soon after his friend died, Luther was caught in a terrible storm. Thinking he would die in that storm, Luther cried out, "Help, beloved Saint Anna! I will become a monk." Luther honored his promise, entering the Augustinian convent at Erfurt two weeks later. But God would not allow Luther to remain an Augustinian monk his whole life.

Luther's sole concern as a monk was to earn a place in heaven. He solemnly vowed a life of poverty and chastity. No one in the convent surpassed Martin Luther in prayer, fasting, and confessing sins. Luther himself observed afterward, "If ever a monk got to heaven by monkery, I would have gotten there."[1] However, none of these pious exercises gave him peace in his soul. He saw sin in everything he did. When he read Scripture, the justice of God terrified him.

In this period of spiritual agony, an old monk, Johann von Staupitz, comforted him. He directed Luther to the gospel and to the forgiveness of sins in Jesus Christ. Staupitz reminded Luther that the law makes known sin, but it cannot heal. The spiritual mentoring of Staupitz directed Luther from his sins to the merits of Christ. Luther began to learn through this spiritual struggle that salvation is not by the works of man, but by the grace of God alone.

Luther's Conversion

During the second year of his monastic life, Luther was ordained into the priesthood. He said his first mass on May 2, 1507. Luther was called by Staupitz from the convent in Erfurt to the convent in Wittenberg. After completing his doctorate in theology, Luther became a professor in the University of Wittenberg. In his lectures Luther treated different books of the Bible: Psalms, Romans, Galatians, Hebrews, and Psalms again. The Psalms and the Epistles to the Romans and Galatians remained his favorite books.

Through his study of Scripture, Luther began to understand and experience the gospel. This came about especially in his newfound understanding of Romans 1:17: "For therein is the righteousness of God revealed from faith to faith: as it is written, The just shall live by faith." For a long time, Luther had been troubled by the concept of God's righteousness. He knew that he could not attain perfection before God. He saw God's righteousness as his burning wrath against those who could not perfectly keep his ways. Therefore, he could not see the gospel in Romans 1:17. Then God opened his eyes. He understood that "the righteousness of God" is the perfect righteousness of Christ, which God imputes to sinners. This righteousness is freely given by faith. A crushing weight was suddenly lifted from Luther's soul. He experienced that he was without sin, not because he did not sin, but because of the freely given righteousness of Christ. This truth brought him the peace he desired in his own heart. By his providential leading, God was preparing Luther to be a reformer of the church, although Luther did not have this intention.

The Ninety-five Theses

Through the course of Luther's early life, God exposed some of the errors of Roman Catholicism to Luther. God exposed the error of works righteousness through Luther's spiritual struggle. When Luther visited Rome at the suggestion of Staupitz, Luther's eyes were opened to the immorality and worldliness of the papacy. Although his faith in the Romish hierarchy was not shaken at the time of his visit, these memories of Rome returned to his mind during the Reformation. Then he had no problem calling the papacy "an institution of the devil."[2]

Another error that concerned Luther in 1517 was the abuse in the sale of indulgences. Indulgences, according to the Roman Catholic Church, removed or reduced the satisfactions required by sinners as a part of penance. The temporal punishment for sin could be removed on the condition of penitence and the payment of money to the church. The Roman Catholic Church led members of the lower classes to believe that they could buy their way into heaven. The sale of indulgences spread to Germany also. John Tetzel, who became a famous orator and seller of indulgences, would prey on the emotions of the lower classes, convincing them to buy indulgences for their departed loved ones. Tetzel approached the Elector of Saxony to request permission to sell indulgences in Saxony. Although the Elector had great confidence in indulgences, he would not allow Tetzel to sell indulgences for fear that this might take too much money from his subjects. So Tetzel set up his business just outside the border of Saxony. Convinced that the sale of indulgences was evil, Luther chose the orderly way of a debate among the monks of the Augustinian order. To open up a public discussion, Luther nailed his Ninety-five Theses to the door of the church at Wittenberg on October 31, 1517.

No one accepted the invitation and no discussion took place. But this did not mean the Theses went unnoticed. The Theses were copied, translated, and circulated throughout Germany and Europe in a few weeks. The Theses, along with other Reformation literature, spread like wildfire throughout Europe. Although Luther wanted only to discuss the issue of indulgences, God used these Theses to begin the Reformation. Luther's fame from the Ninety-five Theses drew him into many other disputations.

Disputations

The printing of the Ninety-five Theses began a war of tracts. Roman Catholic scholars wrote publicly against Luther's Theses. But their defense was weak because they could not defend indulgences from Scripture. Luther responded directly and indirectly to his opponents from the pulpit and with the pen.

The controversy over Luther's views led to a disputation in a large hall in Leipzig from June 27 to July 15, 1519. The main debaters were Martin Luther and John Eck. Eck was a skilled, conceited, and ruthless debater. Although Luther was not a skilled debater, he greatly surpassed Eck in the knowledge of Scripture. The debate between Luther and Eck turned chiefly on the subject of authority. With his skillful debating techniques, Eck drove Luther to positions that he had not previously held. For example, Luther denied the infallibility of church councils and the final authority of the papacy. Because of these denials, Eck charged Luther with being a Hussite. Luther admitted that Hus held some scriptural views and was unjustly condemned and burnt to death. Therefore, from a formal point of view, Eck won the debate.

These debates were important in the history of the Reformation for two reasons. First, Luther gained many followers from these debates. Second, under the providential hand of God, Luther stood on the sole authority of Scripture, which became one of the great *solas* of the Reformation.

Diet of Worms

After the Leipzig Disputation, John Eck returned to Rome calling for the condemnation of Luther and his followers. In June of 1520, the bull of excommunication was completed in Rome. This bull called for the burning of all Luther's books and tracts. But Luther returned fire for fire by publicly burning the bull in the streets of Wittenberg. This burning signified the complete break between Luther and Rome.

In 1521 the Diet of Worms was called by Emperor Charles V to settle the problems that arose from Luther's new teachings. The ruling princes of the provinces of Germany and some Romish officials were present at this Diet. Charles V summoned Luther to this meeting with the guarantee of safe travel to and from the meeting. Luther's friends remembered that Rome had given John Hus the same promise and did not honor that promise. They urged Luther not to attend. However, Luther insisted on going for the cause of Christ.

Luther was not given an opportunity to defend his teachings, but was simply asked if the books lying on the table before him were his. After acknowledging they were his, he was asked if he would recant what he taught. Being unprepared for the question, Luther asked for a day to consider his answer and the emperor granted his request. When asked the same question the next day, part of Luther's well-known answer was, "My conscience is bound in the word of God: I can not and will not recant any thing, since it is unsafe and dangerous to do any thing against the conscience. Here I stand. I cannot do otherwise. God help me! Amen."[3]

The emperor upheld the promise of safe conduct. But Frederick, Luther's elector, afraid that Luther would be captured, had Luther taken secretly to the castle at Wartburg, where Luther stayed for eleven months.

Luther's Life

Convinced of the error of his monastic views, Luther married Katherine von Bora, whom he often called, "Kitty, my rib." She was a hardworking woman who served the constant stream of guests in their home while rarely having enough money. To Martin and Katherine were born three daughters and three sons, but two of the daughters died when they were young. The home of Luther was filled with spiritual activities: prayer, Bible study, and theological discussions. God brought reformation even to Luther's family life.

At the age of sixty-three, Luther traveled to the city of his birth, Eisleben. There he died on February 17, 1546. During the last years of his life, Luther suffered from many ailments.

But in life and in death Luther trusted in his heavenly Father. Through his life and work God laid the foundation of the Reformation. The true church continues to give thanks to God for the work of this reformer.

2

John Calvin: Pastor and Teacher

Barry Gritters

> And he gave some, apostles; and some, prophets; and some, evangelists; and some, pastors and teachers; For the perfecting of the saints, for the work of the ministry, for the edifying of the body of Christ (Eph. 4:11, 12).

GREAT GIFT TO THE CHURCH OF JESUS CHRIST GOD GAVE in John Calvin. Great example for pastors is this unusual man, fit by providence to serve God's church at such a time. Great inspiration for all God's people, young people too, is Calvin, whose dedication and patient love for his fellow saints will move to tears. Truly, God gave him, pastor and teacher, for the perfecting of saints, the work of the ministry, the building up of the body of Christ.

Calvin was born in 1509, the fourth child of a church lawyer and his wife, in Noyon, France, a walled city of about 10,000 residents. Such were the times in the sixteenth century that the likelihood of surviving childhood was not good. Two of Calvin's brothers died in infancy. When he was three Calvin's mother passed away, and his stepmother raised him with his older brother Charles, younger brother Antoine, and two stepsisters.

His early education was the finest, manipulated as it was by his lawyer-father, financed by wages for church positions that he had obtained for Calvin, but which required no work.

Then at age fourteen Calvin had opportunity to study with his friends, sons of a local bishop, in Paris under world-renowned scholars. He never returned to stay in Noyon, the city of his birth.

Originally, his father destined Calvin for theology and the priesthood. When his father saw that wealth was more likely in the practice of law, he directed his son in that way. Unconverted, according to his own confession, Calvin did not object, and he studied. Only later Calvin returned to the study of theology.

The Reformation was barely a few years old when Calvin was a boy. Zwingli was writing and preaching the truth. Erasmus had translated the New Testament. Ministers whose names are unknown to us were preaching the Reformed faith from the Scriptures. By this preaching the Lord was changing hearts. Pope and bishops were angry at the changes. Nations were warring. Because church and state were so closely connected, the church was at the center. In the midst of this turmoil, God was preparing the young man Calvin to be a tireless scholar, an eloquent preacher, a brilliant theologian, a passionate warrior for the faith, and a humble pastor.

First, God would convert him. "God by a sudden conversion subdued my mind," he confessed.[1] From then on, his passion was boundless for the cause of Jesus Christ. Until his death this great gift of God to the church served as an example for pastors today.

Are there young men reading this? Be encouraged, brethren, by the great joy this man found in suffering for the church of Christ as a pastor, and let these lessons from his life teach us about what it means to be a good pastor. Rather than learn of Calvin from a chronological study of his life, let us see five areas of Calvin's ministry that illustrate for us what kind of man, pastor, and teacher, God made him to be.

Willing, in the Day of God's Power

Like other pastors in God's church, God called Calvin to work where he had not chosen. Calvin had been committed to a quiet life of private study. But God dragged him, Jonah-like, to the center of the Reformation battle and the life of the church in a hostile city. Thrust into a position he did not seek, did not want, indeed, ran from, he found himself as a pastor in Geneva, Switzerland.

In 1536 at twenty-seven years old, when he was traveling back from his birthplace, where he had gone to settle the family estate after his father's death, war forced him to take a long detour that led him to the beautiful Swiss town of Geneva. Here, he planned to lodge for the night and be off in the morning to return to Strasbourg to write and study in peace. But God would have nothing of this. William Farel and Pierre Viret, two pastors by whom God began reform in Geneva, looked him up and so pressed him to stay and help them in the work that he at last could not decline their "call." So began a lifetime of self-denying but massively rewarding labor in the public pastorate among Christ's sheep.

After two years of "exile," when Calvin was asked to return to Geneva, he wrote to his colleague Farel, "When I remember that I am not my own, I offer up my heart, presented as a sacrifice to the Lord...I submit my will and my affections subdued and held fast, to the obedience of God."[2] To colleague Viret, about the same call he wrote: "There is no place under heaven of which I can have a greater dread."[3] The decision was not pleasant, but God's will was clear. He went back to Geneva. "I shall follow wherever God leads, who knows best why He has laid this necessity upon me."[4]

Does a young man today run from the pastorate, try to ignore the thoughts God plants, even feel terrified at the possibility of the work of the ministry? So did John Calvin. Remember, though, these two truths: you cannot run from the Lord forever, and he will make you willing and joyful (Ps. 110:3) in the day he stops you from running.

Capable, with the Spirit's Gifts

The man God mastered to be the theologian and organizer of the Reformation, to carry through what Luther began, was a bright and capable young man. Natural gifts that the Lord gave him were developed by a disciplined effort throughout his youth, so that his mind matured to be penetrating and his capacity for learning and memorizing became remarkable.

He learned the languages. Rising early each day to study, to his native French he added Latin, Greek, and Hebrew, and learned them so that he was fluent in them. His grammar was impeccable. Logic and law were in his repertoire. Philosophy and history became familiar friends. Then, because God gave him rare memory and mind, he not only could recall most of what he read, but could grasp the big picture of God's revelation in Scripture and the history of the church in the world. He had natural gifts, indeed, but they were gifts that were developed through arduous work—the kind of work that should be required in today's good, Christian school.

The church needs scholars. Yes, the Lord does use men with few gifts. Most pastors have received from their Maker only a modest portion. Although the Lord of the church likely will not give us very many Calvins again, God's church needs capable men to step forward to do the kind of work in which Calvin engaged. What kind of influence would he have had, had he not known history, and been unfamiliar with the church fathers and councils? Who would have listened to a Calvin who used sloppy grammar? What bishops and other enemies of the faith would have been silenced in a debate by a man whose mind was weak and whose logic was unclear? The church needs scholars. The people of God must pray for them. Perhaps they ought to press, as did Farel and Viret, the young men who are pious and gifted to consider the ministry.

Young men, even if no one presses you, God calls you to use your gifts for his cause. Are you seeking first the kingdom? Perhaps in the ministry of the gospel?

Apt to Teach

The exceptional gift that Jesus Christ gave to Calvin was an aptitude to teach the people. Reading his writing, one immediately senses his unique ability to make clear what is difficult. To this aptitude Christ added a heartfelt desire. The Lord gave Calvin a heart to teach the people. A first-rate theologian, Calvin was interested in showing the light of truth to the common folk. So his first main work, his relatively brief 1536 edition of *Institutes of the Christian Religion* was an attempt to reach the common member of the church.

Calvin's heart yearned to free the people from the bondage of their ignorance, to deliver them from the soul-terrorizing errors of Rome. For this, his instruction was antithetical, exposing in Luther-like fashion the folly of sacramentalism and the dead-end errors of works-righteousness. When he taught, the people heard from Scripture the truth of God's law, the believer's liberty, the Christian life, worship and images, prophecy and eschatology, and the magistrates. They learned what it meant to be joyful, obedient believers in God's wide world.

If the church today will prosper, will help the people of God to live in this late and evil day, she must have pastors who are teachers, who ask the question, as one pastor I know always asked himself as he took his walks, "How can I make this clear to the people of God?" She must train men who yearn with the heart of Calvin (Christ's own heart in him!) for a people who know the truth.

Humble and Modest

Gifts without wisdom are worthless. Ability in a proud man is dangerous. The church has found too often, to her great sorrow, that if the Lord does not mix in wisdom and humility, modesty and selflessness, a man with few gifts is far preferable than the man who towers with ability but is arrogant.

The man God gave to the church from 1509 to 1564 was

blessed with a sincere, selfless desire to serve Jesus Christ. Without pretense, desiring nothing more than the honor of his master, John Calvin humbly served his Savior. Part of humility is a willingness to confess one's faults. Although Calvin struggled with acknowledging weaknesses like anyone else, the Lord gave him that gift as well. More than once he apologized to the city council (church and city government were tightly bound together in those days) for his quick temper and what he considered unrighteous anger. Also, when he and Farel were riding out of Geneva, expelled from their pastorates because pastors and city council could not agree, Calvin wanted to discuss the possibility that they had been less than wise in exerting the pressures for change. It is doubtful that their expulsion came because of lack of judgment, but the desire to examine himself and to be open to the prospect is commendable.

The reformer had no interest in money and possessions, another necessary quality in pastors. His humility showed itself in a complete lack of desire for material things. Content with the barest necessities, Calvin would reject raises, return salary, refuse gifts, and often use part of his meager salary for the French refugees in Geneva. Once, when the other ministers asked Calvin to seek a raise for them, Calvin suggested to the city council that they lower his salary and give the difference to the other, poorer pastors.

The reputation of the reformer as completely disinterested in money reached the pope. When Calvin died, Pope Pius IV said, "The strength of that heretic consisted in this,—that money never had the slightest charm for him."[5] Cardinal Sadoleto, one of Calvin's chief antagonists, visited Geneva incognito to see the famous Protestant. When he knocked on Calvin's modest apartment door, he was astounded that Calvin himself answered the door, and not one of his servants who he assumed would have been scurrying about doing his master's bidding. The most famous man in Protestantism lived in a little house, answering his own door.

Let every aspirant to the ministry pray for such a spirit! And may God give the church such pastors!

Steadfast under Pressures

Probably the most wonderful grace given to Calvin was the grace of endurance in severest trials. What an example of a man of God who sacrificed himself for the church of Christ. No fool who sought a martyr's death, Calvin fled threats more than once, biding his time until he could return and be useful for God's kingdom. Yet the reformer was willing to endure all things for Christ's sake.

He was chased from his own pulpit, threatened with swords on the streets, and driven from Geneva. Guns were fired outside his bedroom window. The very council who had called him to Geneva opposed him and had his friends punished for protecting him. His dear friend and colleague, the blind pastor Claudet, was poisoned for standing for the truth. Evil rumors were spread thick and far about Calvin. For the sake of the ministry, he risked his own life visiting the sick, and he ministered to many at his own expense. Only one of his physical ailments would have driven most pastors to a bed of rest; Calvin endured, without complaint, a dozen. His own testimony was that he went twenty years without letup from headaches. He suffered arthritis, gout, malaria, and finally five years of tuberculosis. One story has a doctor recommending Calvin gallop hard on a horse to dislodge his kidney stones, but his hemorrhoids were so severe he could not bear to ride.

Yet he continued to labor untiringly for the cause of the One who delivered him from so great a death, and would yet deliver him. When friends begged him to rest and recover, he responded, "What? Would you want the Lord to find me idle when He comes?" None of this troubled the man of God, whose love for Christ and vision of his reward spurred him on to unceasing labor for the cause of God who, Calvin said, "drew me out of the abyss...to the light of the gospel...He has so far extended His mercy towards me as to use me and my work to announce the truth of His gospel. He will show Himself the Father of so miserable a sinner."[6]

After his fifty-five-year-old colleague Calvin passed away,

Farel, now in his seventies, said to the group of friends gathered at the deathbed, "Oh, what a glorious course he has happily finished."[7]

Lord of thy beloved church, make us and fit us to be such servants of thine! Raise up men for us with such hearts, offered promptly and sincerely to thee.

3

Luther's Only Truly Congenial Disciple

David J. Engelsma

FAMED LUTHER-SCHOLAR KARL HOLL REGARDED JOHN Calvin as "Luther's only truly congenial disciple."[1] This high estimation of Calvin shocked the Lutherans, who have always nursed a grudge against Calvin and Calvinists. It might have surprised Luther, who was inclined to lump Calvin with the despised "sacramentarians."

Luther and Calvin were contemporaries, although Calvin was twenty-six years younger than Luther. For about ten years, until Luther's death in 1546, they labored together on behalf of the Reformation, Luther in Germany and Calvin in Geneva and Strasbourg.

They never met. They did not even correspond. The closest contact that Calvin had with Luther was Calvin's friendship with Melanchthon, Luther's colleague in Wittenberg.

Luther knew of Calvin. On two occasions, Luther spoke well of Calvin. In a letter to Martin Bucer, a common friend (at those times when Luther was not incensed with Bucer), Luther wrote: "Please greet reverently Mr. John Sturm and John Calvin; I have read their books with special pleasure."[2] Melanchthon once reported to Calvin that Luther had referred to Calvin as "a gifted man"—praise that pleased Calvin immensely.

Nevertheless, Luther's violent condemnation of all who denied a physical presence of Christ's body and blood in the

Luther's Only Truly Congenial Disciple

bread and wine of the Lord's supper—the "sacramentarians"—fell also on Calvin. It is likely that Luther intended his condemnation to reach Calvin. And Calvin felt the sting of the great reformer's diatribe.

On his part, Calvin esteemed and praised Luther highly. He was well aware of Luther's serious weaknesses, especially his furious outbursts against those who differed with his doctrine of the Lord's supper. David Steinmetz observes: "While Calvin agreed with Luther that the defense of the truth required theologians to engage in polemical discussions…he could not agree with the ferocity of Luther's attacks on other Protestant reformers…or overlook the self-indulgent character of Luther's piques and rages."[3] In response to one such outburst by Luther, Calvin wrote, "I am thoroughly ashamed of him [Luther]," although he prefaced the remark with the words, "From my heart I reverence him."[4]

Despite Luther's assaults upon him for his doctrine of the Lord's supper, Calvin continued to hold Luther in the highest esteem. In 1544 (two years before his death), in the work, "Short Confession of the Lord's Supper," Luther savaged the Swiss, Calvin, and even Melanchthon for their views of a spiritual presence of Christ in the supper. Calvin reacted in a letter to Bullinger of Zurich: "Often have I been wont to declare, that even although he were to call me a devil, I should still not the less hold him in such honour that I must acknowledge him to be an illustrious servant of God. But while he is endued with rare and excellent virtues, he labours at the same time under serious faults."[5]

According to David Steinmetz, "Among the non-Lutheran theologians of the sixteenth century, none was more reluctant to disagree with Martin Luther or more eager to find common ground with him than John Calvin."[6]

Calvin's esteem for Luther was not hero-worship. It was not even the Christian virtue of respect for a great man of God in spite of his flaws. Calvin esteemed Luther highly because Calvin was "Luther's only truly congenial disciple." Calvin saw that Luther was the man whom Christ had chosen to recover the gospel for his church. This was why Calvin, always careful with his words, could refer to Luther as an "apostle." The fundamental doctrine of the gospel that Luther recovered, Calvin embraced, taught, developed, and handed over to the church that would follow. Thus Calvin promoted the essential work of Martin Luther on behalf of God and his church. Only Calvin laid hold of Luther's fundamental doctrine and promoted Luther's essential work.

The fundamental doctrine of Martin Luther was the glory of God in Jesus Christ in the salvation of elect sinners by free, almighty grace, apart from the works, worth, and will of these sinners. Luther believed this truth with all his heart and confessed it with a prodigious outpouring of mouth and pen. He believed it because this truth is God's own word about himself, Holy Scripture. "[Salvation] is not of him that willeth, nor of him that runneth, but of God that sheweth mercy" (Rom. 9:16). This doctrine exposed the Roman Catholic Church as a false church, and destroyed it. This doctrine reformed the true church, which had been corrupted by the lie that God will try to save those who show themselves worthy, and established her—in genuine Protestantism—as the glorious, indestructible kingdom of God in the world.

The specific denial of God's sovereignty in salvation that prevailed at the time was the false teaching that a sinner becomes righteous before God by his own good works. Therefore, Luther, who always practiced the rule that one must defend the truth at the precise point where it is presently being attacked, emphasized justification by faith alone. The justified sinner is righteous before God apart from any work of his own, including the good works that faith produces and faith itself as a good work.

Luther's emphasis was a righteousness for guilty humans consisting only of the obedience of Jesus Christ in his life and death. But his fundamental doctrine was God's sovereign grace in the salvation of elect sinners. Because the divine sovereignty in salvation was his fundamental doctrine, Luther taught election and its necessity.

> On your view [says Luther to a defender of the heresy that God merely helps willing people to save themselves], God will elect nobody, and no place for election will be left; all that is left is freedom of will to heed or defy the long-suffering and wrath of God. But if God is thus robbed of His power and wisdom in election, what will He be but just that idol, Chance, under whose sway all things happen at random? Eventually, we shall come to this: that men may be saved and damned without God's knowledge! For He will not have marked out by sure election those that should be saved and those that should be damned; He will merely have set before all men His general long-suffering, which forbears and hardens, together with His chastening and punishing mercy, and left it to them to choose whether they would be saved or damned, while He Himself, perchance, goes off, as Homer says, to an Ethiopian banquet![7]

Because Luther taught biblical election, he taught that the eternal decree appointing some to salvation included the ordaining of the others to damnation. Luther taught eternal, sovereign reprobation: "God...of His own mere will abandon[s], harden[s] and damn[s] men."[8]

In their perceptive "Historical and Theological Introduction" to their translation of Luther's *The Bondage of the Will*, Packer and Johnston call attention to Luther's fundamental doctrine.

> The doctrine of free justification by faith only...is often regarded as the heart of the Reformers' theology, but this is hardly accurate. The truth is that their thinking was really centred upon the contention of Paul...that the sinner's entire salvation is by free and sovereign grace only. The doctrine of justification by faith was important to them because it safeguarded the principle of sovereign grace; but it actually expressed for them only one aspect of this principle, and that not its deepest aspect...To the Reformers, the crucial question was not simply, whether God justifies believers without works of law. It was the broader question, whether sinners are wholly helpless in their sin, and whether God is to be thought of as saving them by free, unconditional, invincible grace, not only justifying them for Christ's sake when they come to faith, but also raising them from the death of sin by His quickening Spirit in order to bring them to faith. Here was the crucial issue: whether God is the author, not merely of justification,

but also of faith; whether, in the last analysis, Christianity is a religion of utter reliance on God for salvation and all things necessary to it, or of self-reliance and self-effort. "Justification by faith only" is a truth that needs interpretation. The principle of *sola fide* is not rightly understood till it is seen as anchored in the broader principle of *sola gratia*.[9]

For Luther, religion is not man-centered, but God-centered. Not man and his happiness (achieved in the final analysis by man himself), but God and his glory (accomplished by God himself) is the heart of the Christian gospel. This is why Karl Holl regarded Calvin not merely as Luther's best disciple but as Luther's only truly congenial disciple. Correctly, Holl was critical of the notion of contemporary scholarship that the formula "seeking the glory of God [is] a Calvinistic concept." "Here too," Holl declared, "Calvin only continued Luther's work."[10]

The only truly congenial disciple of Luther was John Calvin.

Where are the truly congenial disciples of Luther and Calvin today?

They are not the Lutherans, most of whom (contrary to their own creed) teach that God's salvation of sinners is dependent upon sinners' choosing Christ by their own free will. The rest teach that God saves those who do not resist, which comes down to the same thing: man is sovereign in salvation. That the Lutherans are not truly disciples of Luther is evident from their embarrassment at Luther's *The Bondage of the Will*.

The true disciples of Luther and Calvin are not the fundamentalists and evangelicals. These are outspoken that salvation depends on man's decision for Christ, that God does not even know who will be saved and lost, and that God exists to make people happy.

Neither are they the majority of the Reformed and Presbyterians. They are no truly congenial disciples of Luther and Calvin who insist that the gospel is God's saving love and earnest desire to save all without exception, which

Luther's Only Truly Congenial Disciple

love and desire are frustrated by the unbelief of many. They are no truly congenial disciples of Luther and Calvin who make faith a condition that the sinner must fulfill in order to make God's general promise effective and thus obtain salvation for themselves. They are no truly congenial disciples of Luther and Calvin who are teaching (albeit coyly and damnably obscurely), and receiving those who are teaching, that sinners are justified by faith and by the good works of faith. They are no truly congenial disciples of Luther and Calvin who, as soon as they hear a good, hearty, consistent confession of the sovereignty of God in salvation and damnation, turn white and gasp, "hyper-Calvinism!" or turn red and protest, "But man is responsible!"

Where are the truly congenial disciples of Luther and Calvin in the twenty-first century?

They exist, as surely as Christ will not let his work in the sixteenth-century Reformation of the church come to nothing.

Wherever they are, there are the gospel and the true church.

4

John Knox: Reformer and Preacher

Dale Kuiper

The man who in the estimation of friend and foe alike was the greatest man that Scotland ever produced was born in 1505 near the village of Haddington (some of his biographers place his birth as late as 1512). John Knox's education was at the Burgh School of Haddington, where the instructors were Roman Catholic and the instruction prepared young men for the clergy or holy orders. Latin was stressed at this school, so much so that the students were required to speak Latin at all times. Knox was an outstanding Latin scholar. He did not study Hebrew and Greek until after his fortieth year. He remained in the Haddington school until he was seventeen, at which time he faced the question of where to attend university. By choosing to remain in Scotland, Knox avoided the humanism that was rampant in the schools on the continent. He finally decided to attend the University of Glasgow, mainly because the most famous teacher in Scotland at that time, John Major, was on the faculty there. This university was a stronghold of Roman Catholic teaching. It sought to defend and advance medieval theology and philosophy as well as the authority of the pope.

Knox was ordained into the priesthood shortly before 1540. He employed himself in giving private instruction to the sons of prominent Scottish families, rather than engaging in parochial duties. It is generally thought that Knox never renounced his priestly vows but considered his original ordination to suffice even as he took up the cause of the Reformation in Scotland.

Knox first professed the Protestant faith toward the end of 1545. Several influences were used by God to convert this peasant's son from the bondage of Rome into the freedom of the gospel of Jesus Christ. In his early manhood he read both Augustine and Jerome. He attended the preaching of George Wishart for some time, became his personal friend, and even served as his bodyguard when Wishart's life was threatened. Knox embraced Wishart's Reformed preaching with enthusiasm. For this preaching, George Wishart was burned at the stake by Cardinal Beaton. Another powerful influence in Knox's conversion was his correspondence with John Calvin and Theodore Beza, and his residence in Geneva on several occasions. At first Knox was nearer to Luther than to Calvin in his views, but later he considered *Lutheran* a term of reproach, agreeing with Hugh Latimer that the German Reformation was only a partial receiving of the truth.[1] Knox's views regarding the papacy, the mass, purgatory, and other outrages show clearly that he embraced the teachings of the Genevan reformers. Along with these three influences we must add Knox's wholehearted commitment to the Bible as the inerrant word of God and as the only, final authority in matters of faith, worship, and life. Knox agreed with a certain Balnaves, whom he quoted:

> They deceive you which say, The Scriptures are difficult, no man can understand them but great clerics. Verily, whom they call their clerics, know not what the Scriptures mean. Fear nor dread not to read the Scriptures as ye are taught here before; and seek nothing in them but your own salvation, and that which is necessary for you to know. And so the Holy Spirit, your teacher, shall not suffer you to err, nor go beside the right way, but lead you in all verity.[2]

Knox expounded the word of God, Old Testament and New, with insight and power. He applied the Scriptures to the situation in Scotland, England, and elsewhere in Europe.

He loved the Psalms and explained them at length to those in spiritual distress with great understanding of them and with compassion for the weak. Another favorite passage was Deuteronomy 4:2, "Ye shall not add unto the word which I command you, neither shall ye diminish ought from it, that ye may keep the commandments of the LORD your God which I command you." This passage was a faithful guide to him in all his difficult labors, as it was to Luther and Calvin. He embraced the great Reformation principle of *sola Scriptura*.

The bold reformer's first charge was at St. Andrews. The first sermon he ever preached had for its text Daniel 7:24, 25. He called the Church of Rome the "Man of Sin, the Antichrist, the Whore of Babylon."[3] He laid down the marks by which the true church may be discerned from the false. Some said, "Others hewed the branches of the papistry, but he strikes at the root to destroy the whole." Others said, "Master George Wishart spake never so plainly, and yet he was burnt; even so will he be."[4]

A short time later the castle of St. Andrews became a refuge for those of Reformed persuasion because Scotland sided with England politically and religiously against the Roman Catholic nation of France. In 1547 a French army invaded Scotland and took Knox and other refugees captive, forcing them to row in the galleys for seventeen months. As a galley slave Knox suffered many torments, and his health was permanently damaged. After his release in 1549, Knox served several churches in England: Berwick, Newcastle, and London. While in London he joined with other pastors in approving "The Articles concerning an Uniformity of Religion," a document which became the basis of the Thirty-nine Articles of the Church of England.

The years 1554-59 found Knox in Europe. He served a congregation of English-speaking refugees in Dieppe, France, and a similar type of congregation in Hamburg, Germany, at Calvin's urging. This pastorate he resigned due to controversies over vestments, ceremonies, and the use of the English prayer book. He next became the pastor of an

English refugee congregation in Geneva. During these years Knox did much writing, for this time in Europe was the most peaceful of his life. Although urged by Bullinger and Calvin to use caution regarding female magistrates, Knox published his *First Blast of the Trumpet against the Monstrous Regiment of Women*. Because Anabaptism was growing in England and in Scotland, a request came from England to the exiles in Geneva that someone write against the attack being made by the Anabaptists against predestination. Knox was chosen to make this response. Understanding the importance of this issue for true religion he wrote,

> But yet I say, that the doctrine of God's eternal Predestination is so necessary to the Church of God, that, without the same, can Faith neither be truly taught, neither surely established: man can never be brought to true humility and knowledge of himself: neither yet can he be ravished in admiration of God's goodness, and so moved to praise him as appertaineth. And therefore we fear not to affirm, that so necessary as it is that true faith be established in our hearts, that we be brought to unfeigned humility, and that we be moved to praise him for his free graces received; so necessary also is the doctrine of God's eternal Predestination...Then only is our salvation in assurance, when we find the cause of the same in the bosom and counsel of God.[5]

Knox's views in the area of ecclesiology are remarkably similar to those of the Protestant Reformed Churches. He thundered against the claims of the papacy. He called the mass an abomination and an idolatry. He considered the preaching of the gospel to be the chief means of grace and the sacraments to be secondary to preaching as a sign and seal. For Knox, baptism was the sign of entrance into union with Christ and thus was to be administered to a person but once, while the Lord's supper was continuous nourishment for believers in Christ. Knox stood for infant baptism and was dead set against any rebaptism; the Anabaptists were his foe not only in the matter of baptism but also because they tried to upset the entire social order.

We find it interesting also that Knox considered Roman

Catholic baptism valid and no reason for rebaptism. While insisting that Romish baptism is an adulteration and profanation of the baptism which Christ instituted, insisting that it leads people to put their confidence in the bare ceremony, and insisting that God's children ought never to offer their children to Romish baptism for this is to offer them to Satan, Knox nevertheless answered the question, "Shall we be baptized again that in our infancy were polluted with that adulterated sign?" with an unqualified "No." His grounds for this position were: first, "The fire of the Holy Ghost has burnt away whatsoever we received at their hands besides Christ Jesus' simple institution"; second, "And in very deed, the malice of the devil could never altogether abolish Christ's institution, for it was ministered to us 'in the name of the Father, of the Son, and the Holy Ghost'"; and third, "I confess, for the time it did not profit us; but now, as is said, the Spirit of Christ Jesus, illuminating our hearts, has purged the same by faith, and makes the effect of that sacrament to work in us without any iteration of the external sign."[6]

Knox held strenuously to the regulative principle of worship as we also know it and maintain it. Condemning the mass, he said,

> And now, in a few words, to make plain that wherein you may seem to doubt: to wit, that God's word damns your ceremonies, it is evident; for the plain and strait commandment of God is, "Not that thing which appears good in thy eyes shalt thou do to the Lord thy God, but what the Lord thy God has commanded thee; that do thou; add nothing to it; diminish nothing from it." Now unless you are able to prove that God has commanded your ceremonies, this his former commandment will damn both you and them.[7]

All religious ceremonies and institutions must have clear biblical warrant if they are to be considered valid expressions of worship. Always Knox's argument against false worship turns upon his defense of the regulative principle of worship.

Only in one respect did Knox differ from the Genevan theologians and Reformed churches today. He never really condemned the episcopacy. He was a man of his time and shared the views of his contemporaries in the matter of church government. His refusal of an English bishopric was for practical rather than principle reasons. He preferred pastoral work in a humble sphere, preaching the blessed evangel, rather than the arduous duties of a superintendent. He never held the opinion that bishops were an unscriptural institution; they could be tolerated. Beza, hearing of the discussions going on in Scotland on church government, wrote to Knox in April of 1572:

> But of this, also, my Knox, which is now almost patent to our very eyes, I would remind yourself and the other brethren, that as Bishops brought forth the Papacy, so will false Bishops (the relicts of Popery) bring in Epicurism into the world. Let those who devise the safety of the church avoid this pestilence, and when in process of time you shall have subdued that plague in Scotland, do not, I pray you, ever admit it again, however it may flatter by the pretence of preserving unity.[8]

It is thought that had he lived longer his attitude would have changed and come more in line with the Presbyterian form of church government.

As a theologian Knox was not equal to Calvin, or even Melanchthon; he lacked the constructive powers needed to build up a theological system that united all doctrines into a unified whole. Nevertheless, he was a formidable, skillful disputant. His preaching style was unyielding and at times harsh. His language could be rather violent. His five conferences with Queen Mary were characterized by language that was exceedingly blunt and was not designed to win her over but to show her how wrong she was. However, he was the gentle father of five children born to him by two wives, the second of which, much younger than he, served as his nurse in his declining years. He was loved by his students and parishioners, and was a good example to them in all godliness. His appearance was grave and severe, although he possessed a natural graciousness and dignity. His love for the truth and boldness in declaring it drew believers to his preaching services. He spent much time and meditation on his sermons, either writing them out in full or using copious notes. Near the end of his life, he was so weak that he had to be helped into the pulpit; once there he became so vigorous that he began to strike the pulpit as to destroy it. His harshness in debate and in preaching was defended by his followers for the importance of the issues at stake; they required a plainspoken prophet rather than a smooth-tongued orator.

The esteem in which Knox was held by the faithful in Scotland was expressed by his servant Richard Ballantyne:

> Of this manner departeth this man of God, the light of Scotland, the comfort of the Kirke within the same, the mirror of Godliness, and patron and example to all true ministers, in purity of life, soundness in doctrine, and in boldness in reproving of wickedness, and one that careth not the favor of men (how great soever they were) to reprove their abuses and sins...What dexterity in teaching, boldness in reproving, and hatred of wickedness was in him, my ignorant dullness is not able to declare.[9]

Knox died in October of 1572, full of faith and still ready for the conflict. He died quietly and in peace, with friends reading to him Isaiah 53 and John 17. He was buried in the graveyard near the church of St. Giles, where a flat stone still marks his grave.

Knox's importance for the cause of the church and gospel of Christ in Scotland, England, and the continent can hardly be overemphasized. He gave his entire life to reformation of the church. His religion took full possession of him, as true religion ought. Just before he died he said of himself, "None have I corrupted; none have I defrauded; merchandise have I not made." Just after he died the Earl of Mortoun eulogized him thus: "Here lieth a man who in his life never feared the face of man: who hath been often threatened with dag and dagger, but yet hath ended his days in peace and honor. For he had God's providence watching over him in a special manner, when his very life was sought."[10]

All Presbyterian and Reformed churches owe a great debt to John Knox and thankfulness to God for what he wrought through this brave man of the hour. Where can men of his stature be found today in Scotland, England, Europe, and the United States? Where can there be found such holy hatred for Romish superstitions, false doctrine, and wickedness today, as could be found in Knox from the time of his conversion to the last day of his life? May God continue to raise up such men for the preservation and defense of the truths of the Reformation today!

5

Calvin and Knox's Relationship of Mutual Love and Esteem

David Higgs

In May of 1554 John Knox came to Geneva where he met John Calvin face to face for the first time. It is apparent that there had been correspondence between the two prior to this time, as Calvin had recommended Knox to Bullinger at least as early as March of the same year.[1]

Knox began this journey to Geneva in January of 1554 when he was forced into exile from England. This was due to the ascension to the throne of the devoted Roman Catholic, Mary Tudor, more popularly known as Bloody Mary because of the persecution she aimed at Protestants upon her ascension.

After some wanderings, but immediately prior to visiting Geneva, Knox traveled through parts of Helvetia, part of modern-day Switzerland, the region from which the Helvetic Confessions are named. In a loving pastoral letter to his afflicted brethren in England, Knox wrote of this time:

> My awne estait is this: since the 28th of Januar, I have travellit through all the congregationis of Helvetia, and hes reasonit with all the Pastouris and many other excellentlie learnit men upon sic matters as now I can not commit to wrytting: gladlie I wold be toung or be pen utter the same to Godis glorie.[2]

It is obvious from this account that, despite the trying circumstances that had forced him from his beloved Scotland and England, Knox must have entered Geneva refreshed after having had his spirits raised by godly fellowship among the Reformed in Helvetia. In this mood and on this occasion, Knox became acquainted with the "celebrated Calvin and an intimate friendship was soon formed between them, which subsisted until the death of Calvin in 1564."[3]

The relationship was one which Knox's biographer, M'Crie, summarized accurately and succinctly when he addressed the mutual respect of the two reformers:

> They were nearly of the same age; and there was a striking similarity in their sentiments, and in the more prominent features of their character. The Genevan reformer was highly pleased with the piety and talents of Knox, who, in his turn, entertained a greater esteem and deference for Calvin than for any other of the reformers.[4]

Strained Relations

While M'Crie's observation is accurate, even the best of friends are not immune to rocky periods in their relationships. The same was true of Calvin and Knox. They had a close friendship. It was a close friendship built upon mutual respect. But there were times when they were not well pleased with each other. The most notable example of this was occasioned by Knox's *First Blast of the Trumpet against the Monstrous Regiment of Women*. This book contains Knox's vigorous views against the rule of women in the civil sphere.

In a letter to William Cecil, the secretary to Queen Elizabeth I of England, Calvin explained how he sympathized theologically with Knox's position, but had explained to Knox in a private conversation:

> Certain women had sometimes been so gifted that the singular blessing of God was conspicuous in them, and made it manifest that they had been raised up by the providence of God...It did not seem proper to

me that this question should be mooted, not only because the thing was odious in itself, but because in my judgment it is not permitted to unsettle governments that have been set up by the peculiar providence of God.[5]

On this basis Calvin went on to pass his most severe criticism of Knox. In the process of explaining why he had been hesitant to criticize the Scottish reformer earlier he wrote:

I had reason to fear, if the affair had been brought to a trial, that for the inconsiderate vanity of one man, an unfortunate crowd of exiles would be driven not only from this city, but from almost every part of the world, especially as the evil now admitted of no other remedy than the exercise of indulgence.[6]

Strong words indeed! But these were the most severe words that occurred in the relationship of these two reformers, and they were written in an era when strong words were more the accepted norm than they are today.

Knox's Regard for Calvin

There are few letters extant that Knox wrote to Calvin. Nevertheless, from a number of sources, we can gain an idea of how Knox regarded the Genevan reformer.

First, Knox had cause to write to Calvin on a number of occasions concerning Knox's desire to reform the worship in the English congregation in Frankfurt. This in itself shows the high esteem he had for his fellow reformer. Further, the extent of his esteem is seen in that Knox followed the advice of Calvin.[7]

Second, Knox's writings are sprinkled with occasional references to Calvin. Although brief, these references show Knox's high regard for the Genevan reformer. An example will serve to illustrate this point. In 1554 Knox wrote "A Godly Letter to the Faithful in London." In this letter, commenting on the need to condemn the idolatry of the Romish mass, Knox writes of Calvin: "Heir is to be observit, as that singular instrument of God, Johne Calvin, maist diligentlie noteth, that the rest of the Prophetis warkis wes writtin in the Hebrew toung."[8]

Also there is the famous pronouncement by Knox concerning Geneva in general but no doubt focused on Calvin in particular. In a letter to his friend Anne Locke he wrote,

> ...in my hart I wald haif wishit, yea and can not cease to wish, that it wold pleas God to gyd and conduct your self to this place, whair I nether feir nor eschame to say is the maist perfyt schoole of Chryst that ever was in the erth since the dayis of the Apostillis. In other places, I confess Chryst to be trewlie preachit; but maneris and religioun so sinceirlie reformat, I have not yit sene in any uther place.[9]

Calvin's Regard for Knox

There is much evidence to show how highly Calvin regarded the Scottish reformer. This comes out in a number of different ways.

First, we can see something of Calvin's love for and esteem of Knox in the letters he wrote to him personally. In one, dated November 7, 1559, the Genevan reformer began with the respectful greeting "most excellent brother." He concluded the same letter:

> Farewell, most excellent sir and our very dear brother. The whole assembly of the pious in our name wish you prosperity; and we pray God that he may govern you all by his Spirit even to the end, sustain you by his power, and shield you with his protection.[10]

In another letter, dated April 23, 1561, Calvin showed his concern for Knox's well-being. Some misunderstanding had occurred between them. Consequently, Calvin was at pains, from the beginning of this letter, to remove any offense Knox may have taken. This he accomplished by giving high praise of Knox's character and concluding with these beautiful words of exhortation and comfort:

> Farewell, distinguished sir and honored brother. May the Lord always stand by you, govern, protect, and sustain you by his power. Your distress for the loss of your wife justly commands my deepest sympathy. Persons of her merit are not often to be met with. But as you have well learned from what source consolation for your sorrow is to be sought, I doubt not but you endure with patience this calamity. You will salute very courteously all your pious brethren. My colleagues also beg me to present to you their best respects.[11]

This same concern for the welfare of Knox is seen also in Calvin's letters to others.[12] He showed concern and also high esteem for Knox's preaching, doctrine, and dedication. In a letter to the Earl of Arran, Calvin wrote:

> I praise God, likewise, Monseigneur, for the care and holy desire which you manifest that the pure doctrine of the gospel should be preached in your nation. To which duty I doubt not but our brother, Master Knox, will willingly dedicate his services, as indeed he has already shown.[13]

And indeed, Calvin's esteem included the writings and scholarship of the Scottish reformer. For "The Epistle Dedicatory" to his *Sermons on Election and Reprobation* he wrote,

> For further satisfaction in this question, I refer all Christians to the Books that are written hereof, and namely to these excellent Sermons: M. Knox hath learnedly answered the objections of the adversaries in a Book printed at Geneva.[14]

From the prince of exegetes, exemplary scholar, and leading reformer, this is high praise, indeed—praise which shows that Calvin and Knox shared a mutual respect and love for each other.

We have seen just a little of the relationship that existed between the leading Scottish and Genevan reformers. They did have their differences. At times these differences led to a degree of anger and the speaking of harsh words. But these two men had a firm conviction of the fundamental, central issues of the gospel which, under God, they were instrumental in teaching and preaching. It was this that cemented their relationship, this love for the full-orbed gospel and the desire to teach and preach it.

We who love the truth of God's word, as it is found in the fundamental doctrines of the Scriptures, ought to learn from Calvin and Knox. Let us roll up our sleeves and work for the cause of God and his kingdom. Let us have a high regard and love for each other, who hold the truth uncompromisingly. Let us, by God's grace, be like Knox and Calvin in our love and esteem for the truth and for all who hold the truth.

Part 2

History

6

The Reform of Geneva

Steven Key

John Calvin's role in the reform of Geneva was divinely ordained. Calvin himself did not seek it. In probably his most lengthy autobiographical sketch, found in the preface to his *Commentary on the Book of Psalms*, he pointed out that he had no intention of staying in Geneva more than a single night, let alone becoming a leading figure there.[1]

Calvin's plan was to go to Strasbourg. His heart was set on a sheltered life of private studies. He ended up passing through Geneva, because in God's wonderful providence the direct road from Paris to Strasbourg was blocked, making it necessary for Calvin to take a much longer, circuitous route to the south. So he arrived in Geneva unannounced. Although only twenty-seven years of age, Calvin was a well-known scholar and teacher by this time, and someone who recognized him made known to Farel that the author of the *Institutio* was in the city.[2]

So the reformer and pastor William Farel became the instrument of God to set Calvin on a different path. Calvin wrote:

> Farel...immediately strained every nerve to detain me. And after having learned that my heart was set upon devoting myself to private studies, for which I wished to keep myself free from other pursuits, and finding that he gained nothing by entreaties, he proceeded to

utter an imprecation that God would curse my retirement, and the tranquility of the studies which I sought, if I should withdraw and refuse to give assistance, when the necessity was so urgent. By this imprecation I was so stricken with terror, that I desisted from the journey which I had undertaken.[3]

A political reformation had already taken place in Geneva, in which the bishop of Savoy had been ousted and then replaced by the rule of the magistrates. Following that political reform, the spiritual reformation of Geneva began to flourish, especially under the leadership of Farel and a colleague in the ministry, Pierre Viret. The council of the city suspended the mass in 1535 and subsequently enacted several laws forbidding the practice of the Roman Catholic religion, requiring the priests to convert, and announcing that the evangelical doctrine now preached in Geneva was indeed the holy doctrine of the truth. These ordinances were followed in the spring of 1536 by the exhortation to all citizens to attend to the sermons in order to hear the true gospel. In other words, the magistrates were attempting by law to bring about a spiritual reformation. In that setting Farel and Viret earnestly preached.

But as would soon be seen, true spiritual reformation cannot come by the imposition of laws. As might be expected, division abounded in the city, and there were many factions that from different perspectives were strong opponents of any spiritual reformation.

True reformation is entirely spiritual, the work of God by the Holy Spirit in the hearts of men. And for such reformation God would have John Calvin play the leading role.

Calvin's work in Geneva began in the summer of 1536. He began his work there as a noted teacher, the author of *Christianae religionis institutio,* the *Institutes of the Christian Religion,* published just a few months earlier.

The task of reform in Geneva was daunting. Calvin understood that such reform would involve reorganizing the church according to the word of God, defending the autonomy of the church in relation to the civil magistrates (itself no easy task), as well as bringing change to the mind-set of the people concerning both doctrine and its effects upon morals and the Christian life.

Calvin turned to the work, recognizing only one hope for accomplishing this humanly impossible task. Such reform could come only by the power of the word of God.

It was not long before Calvin "was compelled by circumstances of controversy in the city ... to add to his teaching commitments the responsibility of public preaching."[4] Thus he became known as a preacher and a pastor, and endeavored with his colleagues, especially Farel and Viret, to establish the church and city upon the foundation of biblical truth.

Four months had scarcely passed when Satan reared with intensity his ugly head in Geneva. There were troubles on two fronts. There was an Anabaptist influence in the city, which would mar the Reformation with extremism. This influence was soon turned away when Calvin and his colleagues thoroughly and publicly refuted, by the word of God, the Anabaptist teachings. From a different front came other assaults upon Calvin and the reformers. There was "a certain wicked apostate, who being secretly supported by the influence of some of the magistrates of the city," stirred up opposition toward Calvin and his fellow reformers.[5] This opposition would soon seem to have the victory in the ouster of both Farel and Calvin from Geneva. The expulsion of God's servants from Geneva on April 22, 1538, less than two years after Calvin had begun his labors in the city, came from a dispute concerning the exercise of Christian discipline. Calvin saw that the biblical exercise of Christian discipline was a critical mark of the true church. He would place discipline alongside the two marks generally recognized by the churches of the Protestant Reformation—faithful preaching and the proper administration of the sacraments. At this time the exercise of discipline fell primarily to the pastors. The city council, however, insisting that discipline was theirs to exercise and knowing Calvin as the leading figure in this ecclesiastical exercise of discipline, found it presumptuous that a foreigner would take to himself and to the other pastors the right to excommunicate "respectable" Genevan citizens. On January 4, 1538, the city council decreed that the Lord's supper not be refused to anyone. As the dispute between the pastors and the council escalated, Calvin and Farel refused to celebrate the Lord's supper. The council in turn ordered them to stop preaching and, when they refused, expelled them from the city. They were given three days to depart. The reform in Geneva would not come easily.

Who would not have supposed that Calvin's and Farel's expulsion from Geneva would have brought an end to the reformation in that city? But Theodore Beza, in recounting the history, wrote,

> On the contrary, the event showed the purpose of Divine Providence by employing the labors of his faithful servant elsewhere, to train him, by various trials, for greater achievements. Also, by overthrowing those seditious persons, through their own violence, the city of Geneva was purged of much pollution. So admirable does the Lord appear in all his works, and especially in the government of his Church![6]

Calvin breathed a sigh of relief at his expulsion. He finally was relieved of the work he never wanted anyway and saw his opportunity to settle into a quiet life of ivory-tower study. His intention, however, was not God's way. His "escape" from Geneva would be only temporary, while God continued to shape him for the continued work of reform there.

From the summer of 1538 to the summer of 1541, Calvin spent three blessed years in Strasbourg. God gave him time for development and gave him further preparation for the work that yet lay before him. Although one might expect that his expulsion from Geneva would make him a bitter man, God spared him from the sin of such an attitude. Because the cause of God's truth and the Reformation was more important than any personal suffering, Calvin continued to seek Geneva's good even from afar. When Cardinal

Sadoleto craftily attempted to win the city back to the cause of Rome by way of a smooth letter addressed to "his dearly beloved brethren, the magistrates, council, and citizens of Geneva," Calvin responded from Strasbourg with a letter, coming to the defense of the Genevan people and the cause of Christ by setting forth clearly the truth of Scripture as the foundation of the Reformation.[7] Calvin also continued correspondence with certain leading figures and church members in Geneva, encouraging them to patient steadfastness in the truth. But in Strasbourg Calvin was given the opportunity to develop his pastoral understanding as well as his preaching, and to discover that progress always tests patience, and that there are times when progress is better made by careful and moderate dealing, and by depending on the work of the Spirit through the word.

By 1541 a political change had again taken place in Geneva, in which the supporters of the reformers again gained the power. The result was an urgent request for Farel, Calvin, and Viret to return to the city. Farel would not be released from the church in Neufchatel. The church in Berne expressed a willingness to let Viret go for a brief period of time to assist the church in Geneva. The Genevese pleaded with Strasbourg for Calvin's release. In spite of the reluctance of the church in Strasbourg, as well as that of Martin Bucer, the Genevese persisted.

Calvin himself had no desire to return, and in fact looked upon such a return with terror. "Not a day passed in which I did not ten times over wish for death," he wrote.[8] But recognizing that the will of God often goes contrary to one's own inclinations and self-interest, and when Bucer himself became convinced that God would have Calvin go and with fervency pointed Calvin to the example of Jonah, Calvin submitted. On September 13, 1541 he returned to labor until his death.

Calvin recounted his labors in Geneva after 1541, "Were I to narrate the various conflicts by which the Lord has exercised me since that time, and by what trials he has proved me, it would make a long history."[9] The trials were innumerable and would undoubtedly have taken Calvin down had he not had such a high view of the sanctity of the call to his office and the authority of the word of God.

All Calvin's labors toward reform in Geneva were rooted in the Scriptures.

His first order of business was to set in order the institute of the church. Calvin demonstrated that not only the doctrines of the church, but also the form of church government, must come from Scripture. He immediately obtained the consent of the Senate in Geneva to a form of ecclesiastical polity that was derived from the word of God, and from which neither ministers nor people should be permitted to depart.[10] A regular presbytery with full ecclesiastical authority was established. Through much strife with the civil authorities, Calvin saw that the church in Geneva maintained her autonomy and particularly the important exercise of Christian discipline in distinction from any civil penalties that would come under the jurisdiction of the magistrate.

Preaching occupied the chief place in the reformation of the church in Geneva. In the Cathedral of St. Peter, where Calvin generally preached, Sunday worship services were held at daybreak, again at 9 A.M., and yet again at 3 P.M. The children were to be brought at noon for instruction. Shorter preaching services were also held on Monday, Wednesday, and Friday mornings.

Much attention was given to teaching that followed the form of a catechism that Calvin had prepared. In addition, knowing the importance of education to the cause of the gospel, Calvin led the promotion of education with the establishment of the Academy of Geneva.

As part of the ecclesiastical ordinances, a diaconate was also established. Calvin himself was instrumental in the establishment of a hospital in Geneva.

John Calvin saw the word of God applying to every aspect of the Christian's life. He was convinced that the power of the gospel in the heart of God's elect would affect their family life, their church life, the handling of their finances, as well as their place in society and any role they would play in governing. But basic to all these is a true and healthy church. It was that above all else to which Calvin gave his attention.

While the reform of Geneva could itself only be limited, the influence of that reform was widespread. The work of the academy continued to spread its influence for the cause of the Reformed faith for decades even following the death of its founder. Also the refugees who had fled to Geneva returned home carrying the Reformed faith with them. From that point of view, the spiritual reform of Geneva was but a microcosm of that mighty work of God throughout the continent of Europe and beyond, as the Spirit of truth continued to guide his church.

7

God's Continuing Controversy with Unchanged Rome

David J. Engelsma

IN MARCH OF 1545, LESS THAN A YEAR BEFORE HE DIED, Martin Luther published the most vehement condemnation of the Roman Catholic papacy that he had ever written, "Against the Roman Papacy, an Institution of the Devil." It was timed to coincide with the opening of the Council of Trent, the Roman Catholic council that was intended to resist the Protestant Reformation. The title itself is condemnation of the Roman Church, inasmuch as the papacy is the Roman Church. But Luther made explicit the condemnation of the church that has the papacy as her head: "devil's synagogue ... the devil's church ... an un-Christian and anti-Christian church, that is, a papal school of scoundrels."[1] God's great scourge of the Roman Catholic Church went to his grave warring against the Church of Rome.

The conflict continues at the beginning of the twenty-first century. The Reformed church has a controversy with Rome. It is the continuation of the war opened up by the Reformation.

It is necessary to remind ourselves of this because the notion prevails in Protestant churches that Rome has changed. Men suppose that since Vatican II, the Roman Catholic council that met from 1963 to 1965, Rome is no longer the enemy of the gospel that once she was. Now it is possible for Protestants to commune and cooperate with Rome.

Lutheran and Anglican churches are conducting official conferences with Rome that have union as a goal. These conferences have already resulted in statements of doctrinal agreement. Protestant churches in the British Isles have recently reorganized their ecumenical setup to include Rome. Reformed churches in the Netherlands swap preachers and priests at worship services. A prominent Roman Catholic lawyer in the United States pleads in *Christianity Today*, a leading evangelical magazine, for cooperation of evangelical Protestants and the Roman Catholic Church in matters of social action.[2] Recently, there have been significant defections to Rome on the part of leading evangelicals and Presbyterians in the United States. And it is common today that neighborhood Bible study groups include staunch Roman Catholics, not as objects of evangelism, but as full, participating members of the class.[3]

Rome has not changed. Although God rebuked her sharply and plagued her severely in his great controversy with her that we know as the Reformation, Rome has proved incorrigible.

Rome continues to carry a huge load of guilt for her persecution and killing of untold thousands of Reformed and Presbyterian saints. To name only two instances, she murdered scores of thousands of Reformed Christians in the Netherlands and perpetrated unspeakable atrocities upon the French Huguenots in the sixteenth and seventeenth centuries. At this very moment, there goes up in heaven a cry from these souls, killed by Rome for the word of God and for their testimony to the truth, "How long, O Lord, holy and true, dost thou not judge and avenge our blood on them that dwell on the earth?" (Rev. 6:10).

Let no one respond that present-day Rome may not be held responsible for those deeds of a bygone age. For, first, Rome has never repented for these sins. Second, Rome today takes the very same stands, such as the absolute supremacy of the pope over church, state, and purgatory, and maintains the very same doctrines, for example, the sacrifice of Christ for sins in the mass, that moved her to slaughter God's people in the sixteenth and seventeenth centuries. Third, corporate responsibility means that a church in the twenty-first century continues to be responsible for the sins she committed in the distant past. Jesus said to the Jerusalem of his day, "Ye slew [Zacharias]," even though Zacharias had been slain hundreds of years earlier by men long dead (Matt. 23:35). Hundreds of years after the deed, God visits the righteous blood of his martyrs upon the apostate church that shed this blood. During all this time, he sees such a church as a bloody church.

When Pope John Paul II visited Chicago a few years ago, I could never see the white-clad, saintly, benevolent old man that millions of others saw. I saw only a man whose garments were drenched with blood, a man whose hands extended in blessing of the multitudes dripped blood, and a man who was drunken with blood—the blood of the saints and the blood of the martyrs of Jesus.[4] This is why, when Reformed ministers in the Chicago area were praying for the pope as a "man of God," I was praying in my congregational prayer, "From the tyranny of the bishop of Rome and all his detestable enormities, O Lord, deliver us."

Rome has not changed.

Her doctrines remain the same. The Roman Catholic Church maintains as her confession the Canons and Decrees of the Council of Trent. This is Rome's official rejection of every distinctive doctrine of the Protestant Reformation. Maintaining this confession, Rome continues to pronounce her official curse upon every church and upon every person that holds the Reformation gospel: "Let him be anathema!"

Consider only two instances of Rome's damning of fundamental Reformed doctrines in these Canons and Decrees. Against the truth that is the cornerstone of the Reformation gospel of salvation, justification by faith alone, Rome declares, "If any one saith, that by faith alone the impious is justified...let him be anathema." Against the doctrine that is the heart of the church, sovereign predestination, Rome inveighs, "If any one saith, that a man, who is born again and justified, is bound of faith to believe that he is assuredly in the number of the predestinate: let him be anathema."[5]

Not only did Vatican II fail to change a single Roman Catholic doctrine, but it also expressly reaffirmed every important Roman doctrine. In the "Dogmatic Constitution on Divine Revelation," the Roman Catholic Church reaffirmed that tradition is an equal authority in the church with Scripture: "It is not from sacred Scripture alone that the Church draws her certainty about everything which has been revealed. Therefore both sacred tradition and sacred Scripture are to be accepted and venerated with the same sense of devotion and reverence."[6]

In the "Dogmatic Constitution on the Church," Rome reaffirmed, among other things, that as head of the church "the Roman Pontiff has full, supreme, and universal power over the Church"; that "it is a holy and wholesome thought to pray for the dead that they may be loosed from sins," that is, to believe the monstrous fiction of purgatory; and that Mary, the mother of Jesus, is to be worshiped and preached ("Let the entire body of the faithful pour forth persevering prayer to the Mother of God...") as "Mediatrix" (this blasphemous title was expressly given Mary by Vatican II).[7]

In the "Decree on the Ministry and Life of Priests," the Roman Catholic Church reaffirmed its teaching that its mass is a repetition of the sacrifice of Christ for the sins of men: "Through the hands of priests...the Lord's sacrifice is offered in the Eucharist in an unbloody and sacramental manner until He Himself returns."[8]

As though to rub the noses of Protestantism in unchanged Roman doctrine, Vatican II deliberately "proposes again" all the past decisions of the Roman Catholic Church on the meritorious works of saints, the intercession of saints in heaven, prayers to the saints, and indulgences granted by the church because of the merits of the saints.[9]

Rome is unchanged in her doctrinal apostasy.

This is the issue between Rome and the Reformed church.

The Sixteenth-Century Reformation of the Church

Our conflict with Rome is theological. It has to do with God's gospel of sovereign grace; with the pure worship of God; with the authority of God in his word, Holy Scripture; with God's one mediator, Jesus the Christ; with God's headship of the church in Jesus.

God has a continuing controversy with the Roman Catholic Church. God has pronounced his decisive "anathema" upon the Roman Catholic Church: "If any man preach any other gospel unto you than that ye have received, let him be accursed" (Gal. 1:9).

Every Reformed church and every member of the Reformed church is committed, by the Reformed confessions, to God's controversy with Rome. In Question 80 of the Heidelberg Catechism, church and believer condemn Roman Catholicism as "a denial of the one sacrifice and passion of Jesus Christ and an accursed idolatry."[10] In Article 29 of the Belgic Confession, they judge the Roman Catholic Church a "false church."[11] Every condemnation by the Canons of Dordt of the teachings of Arminianism is a condemnation as well of Rome. For Rome's gospel too is a message of salvation by the "free will," the working, and the worth of man.

If a Reformed church has no controversy with Rome, the reason is not that Rome has changed, but that this Reformed church has changed. Doctrinally, she is one with Rome. She has made her peace with Rome's rebellion against God. Reunion with Rome will follow. God has a controversy also with such a Reformed church.

The Reformed church worthy of the name, the church faithful to the sole authority of Scripture and to the gospel of salvation by grace alone, cannot but have a controversy with Rome. God has summoned her to the battle under the banner of his own name. She engages in the controversy in a spiritual manner—by the word—not by earthly force and political action. She instructs her own people thoroughly in the truths of the Reformation gospel. She sharply and clearly exposes the Roman errors. She refuses to have any communion with Rome in ecumenical organizations, in local services of worship, or in cooperative ventures of social action. She warns Reformed people against an unequal yoke with Rome, especially in marriage. She engages in evangelism with Roman Catholics, calling them away from the pope to Christ. And in the end she will once again suffer at Rome's hands, as the Lord foretold in his answer to the martyrs' cry in heaven: "Rest yet for a little season, until [your] fellow servants also and [your] brothers ... should be killed as [you] were." (Rev. 6:11).

Why there must be controversy with Rome, and what the controversy is, the aged Luther pointed out in his parting blast against Rome. In the midst of all the invective, vitriol, and vulgarity of "Against the Roman Papacy," Luther wrote, with unerring insight into the real issue to the very end:

> Here it is firmly forbidden to preach or hear human teachings in the church, for they do not give honor and glory to God, but instead seduce people away from the faith and seek the glory of man. For God alone would speak, work, and govern in his church, so that he alone is glorified, which we have, praise God, managed to achieve in our churches.[12]

8

The History of Anabaptism

Herman Hanko

THE REFORMATION OF THE SIXTEENTH CENTURY WAS A mighty work of God by which the church of Christ was preserved through church reformation. To the student of history, it never ceases to be a wonder how God brought about this Reformation and kept it on a steady biblical course. Not only were the reformers giants of theology who successfully combated the errors of Rome in doctrine, worship, church government, and the Christian life, but they also successfully steered the church away from radical movements which threatened the Reformation almost from the beginning.

These radical movements joined themselves to the Reformation and seemed at first to have an important role in the battle against Romish error. But they were intent on leading Protestantism in a direction wholly contrary to Scripture. It would have been easy and was often tempting to the reformers to incorporate such radical movements within biblical Protestantism. To reject them splintered the churches of the Reformation badly and opened the reformers to the charge that by abandoning the authority of the pope they tore to pieces the unity of the church of Christ. And so often these radical movements seemed to be standing for all the right things.

Nevertheless, part of the wonder of God's work is that the reformers succeeded in opposing Rome on the right and the radical Anabaptist movement on the left.

The Anabaptist movement at the time of the Reformation was an extremely diverse movement.[1] Although all Anabaptists agreed on certain ideas, they disagreed violently on other issues. And within the separate branches of the movement, controversies led to many schisms and splinter groups. For our purposes, we will divide the movement into three branches.

Carlstadt and the Zwickau Prophets

The Lutheran Reformation reached a climax at the Diet of Worms when Martin Luther, the fearless reformer of Germany, stood alone and defenseless before the emperor of the Holy Roman Empire, the princes of Germany, and the higher prelates and theologians of the Roman Catholic Church to take his stirring stand on the basis of the word of God. After the Diet, Luther found refuge for a while in a castle at Wartburg.

During Luther's stay in Wartburg, certain men within the Lutheran camp began to push their radical ideas in Wittenberg. They were dissatisfied with the slow progress of the Reformation, especially in purging the church of the remaining elements of Roman Catholicism: vestiges of the mass, pictures, icons, altars, monkery, colored-glass windows, and such things. Without Luther's calm guiding hand on the tiller, they saw their opportunity to destroy all the hated elements of Romish practices. They unleashed in the city a wave of iconoclasm. Their followers went through the city and into the churches smashing everything that displeased them and introducing practices that, while in keeping with Reformation ideals, were being introduced slowly by Luther as he sought to bring the people to an understanding of the word of God. The radical leaders were Andreas Carlstadt and Justus Jonas.

They were soon joined by men from Zwickau led by Nicholas Storck, Marcus Stubner, and Thomas Muntzer.

These "Zwickau prophets," as they came to be called, were radicals who combined an inward mysticism with a destructive radicalism. They relied heavily on dreams, visions, and direct revelations; they rejected infant baptism; they were chiliastic, that is, they were of the opinion that the millennium had dawned and that it was their calling to establish the millennial kingdom of Christ here on earth. Wittenberg was in an uproar, and hasty and urgent letters were sent to Luther to stop the stampede.

While the elector forbade Luther to return, fearing for his life, Luther felt compelled to return to Wittenberg and, in a series of eight powerful sermons preached on eight successive days, put all the radicals to flight and restored the peace of the city. It was a remarkable demonstration of Luther's powerful pulpit preaching and a proof of his contention that the Reformation could not be accomplished by rioting and insurrection, but only by the power of the word of God. Muntzer was later instrumental in the Peasants' Uprising and died at the hands of the armies sent out to quell the insurrection.

The Munster Debacle

The Reformation had come early to what is now the Netherlands, and Anabaptism had been introduced into the Lowlands by Melchior Hofman as early as 1530. Hofman was a strange man and an erratic thinker. He also was strongly chiliastic, expected momentarily the return of Christ, and relied heavily on special revelations. He made use of fanciful and allegorical interpretations of Scripture to promote his views.

But two men, followers of Hofman, introduced what was the most radical form of Anabaptism on the continent into the Netherlands. They were Jan Matthys, who claimed to be Enoch, and Jan of Leyden, who claimed to be King David. Accepting all the strange views of Hofman, they determined to establish the kingdom of heaven, with its center in German city of Munster, which they called the New Jerusalem. They reached the pinnacle of their power in 1535 and 1536 when, within the walls of Munster, a community was established that practiced adult baptism and community of goods and wives and relied more upon revelation through special visions given the leaders than through the words of Christ in Holy Scripture.

The city was attacked by the forces of the emperor, overcome, and destroyed, with the citizens put to flight or death. The horrible experiment of this radical wing of Anabaptism lasted only a short time.

This fanatic branch of Anabaptism was condemned by other Anabaptists, even in the Lowlands. The successors of the Anabaptists, without the fanaticism of Munster, were followers of Menno Simons. These were the beginnings of what today is known as the Mennonite Church.

The Belgic Confession, which often mentions Anabaptist errors, was written with the Anabaptists of the Lowlands in mind, including the followers of Menno Simons. The views of Menno Simons receive special attention in Article 18, for it was Menno Simons who taught that the human nature of Christ did not come from Mary.[2]

The Swiss Brethren

The wing of Anabaptism that went under the name of "The Swiss Brethren" was the least radical of all. It repudiated the violent excesses of the Zwickau Prophets especially and the followers of Jan of Leyden.

The movement had its beginning in Zurich. In this city Ulrich Zwingli was pressing his reformatory work. Here too, certain men were not satisfied with a slow reformation and were impatient with those who counseled carefulness. The chief leaders were Conrad Grebel (often considered the founder of Anabaptism), Felix Manz, George Blaurock,

Simon Stumf, and Balthasar Hubmaier.[3] Zwingli, in keeping with current views on the relation between church and state, wanted the city council of Zurich to be in control of reform.

When the council decided in favor of Zwingli and his followers at a public disputation in October of 1523, the men who had opposed him separated themselves from the Swiss reformer to establish their own party.

While the immediate issue was the question of the speed of reform and the support of the magistracy, other issues soon arose. In rejecting the control of the council in reformation, these men went further and established the principle of separation between church and state. But the defense of this position led to more radical positions. Grebel denied the propriety of Christians going to war, the use of the civil courts in matters of dispute among Christians, and the legitimacy of the oath for Christians.[4]

The goal of this movement was the establishment of a Christian community, separate from the world, in which the principles of the kingdom of heaven, especially as outlined in the Lord's Sermon on the Mount, were practiced.

The question of believer's baptism, in distinction from the doctrine of infant baptism, came almost immediately to the fore. Believer's baptism was first introduced by Wilhelm Reublin, a pastor of a church in a village near Zurich. The Anabaptists rejected infant baptism partly they could find no New Testament proof for it and partly because they considered infant baptism to be an innovation brought into the church by the antichristian Roman Catholic Church. This denial of infant baptism became the one great issue between Anabaptists and the other branches of Protestantism.

When the Anabaptists were expelled from Zurich, they gathered as a hunted handful of people. At this meeting Blaurock begged Grebel to baptize him with "true Christian baptism." This was done, and Blaurock then proceeded to baptize the others in the group. From that time on, no children were baptized and all baptized adults were rebaptized. (*Anabaptism* means rebaptism.)

In the decades following, the Anabaptists became evangelists who traveled throughout Europe spreading their views. They found ready ears in many places, and Anabaptism became a constant thorn in the side of the true Reformation.

The price the Anabaptists had to pay was great. They were hunted, imprisoned, tortured, and killed. They met in private homes, woods, and caves. They suffered untold hardship. They were put on the rack, roasted in the fire, drowned in rivers and lakes, beheaded, tortured almost beyond endurance. Yet their views continued to spread.

Closely connected with their views on believer's baptism was their position of a pure church, their emphasis on holiness and godliness in life, and their opposition to any support of the secular magistrates in ecclesiastical affairs.

Other doctrinal aberrations soon appeared in their thinking. They considered the sacraments to be of mere symbolic value. In keeping with all baptistic thought, they considered the Old Testament to be so distinct from the New that it was of lesser authority than the New for Christians. Some practiced community of goods in an effort to restore the church to the purity of apostolic times. This was especially true of the Anabaptists in Moravia, who, under the leadership of Jacob Hutter, founded the Hutterites. Hans Denck, an Anabaptist in southern Germany, anticipated later Arminian thought with his teaching that the atonement of Christ was universal in its scope, although efficacious only for the elect.

Because the denial of infant baptism was the one great doctrinal point that united all Anabaptists, this doctrine received the most attention from the reformers. In Switzerland especially, the doctrine of the covenant of grace, with its corollary in the unity of the Old and New Testaments, was first developed under the leadership of such men as Zwingli, Bullinger, and Myconius. This too is a remarkable demonstration of God's wise providence in using error to promote the cause of the truth. Between the extreme of Anabaptism and the corruption of Rome, the reformers had to steer their way. That they did so successfully is due to the sovereign grace of the Holy Spirit of Christ, who leads the church into all truth.

9

The Enemy on the Left

David J. Engelsma

Anabaptists?

Who are they?

And does a Reformed church have to bother itself with them?

Are they such a threat to the Reformation faith in the twenty-first century as to warrant a sharp warning against their errors?

Reformed people must know that the Anabaptist heresy is alive and well. Indeed, it is thriving as never before. Of the two great foes of the faith of the Reformation in history, Roman Catholicism and Anabaptism, the latter is by far the more serious danger to the faith today. Every Reformed Christian worthy of the name is on his guard against Rome. But many are swept away, almost unawares, by the seductions of Anabaptism.

Part of the problem is that the people do not know that the great Reformation of the sixteenth century had to struggle to the victory of a sound, truly Reformed church against enemies on the left as well as against the enemies on the right. The foe on the right was Rome. The foe on the left was Anabaptism. Historians have wrongly called the Anabaptists "the left wing of the Reformation." This name is wrong because it describes the Anabaptists as part of the Reformation movement itself. Although the Anabaptists followed Luther and Zwingli out of the Roman Catholic Church, they were not part of the movement. Immediately after leaving Rome, they also separated from the Reformation churches. They went out, as John writes in 1 John 2:19, that they might be made manifest that they were not of the Reformation.

The Anabaptists were not "the left wing of the Reformation" but the enemies of the Reformation on the left. They were not the "radical Reformation" but a radical departure from the Reformation.

The reformers regarded them as worse enemies than Rome. Luther declared that the Anabaptists were further removed from the gospel than Rome and that if he had to choose he would rather return to Rome than become Anabaptist. The reformer of Scotland, John Knox, agreed. In his "A Warning against the Anabaptists," he wrote:

> But of the other sort [the Anabaptists]...the craft and malice of the Devil fighting against Christ is more covert, and therefore more to be feared; for under the color and cloak of mortification of the flesh, of godly life, and of Christian justice, they have become privy blasphemers of Christ Jesus...and manifest enemies to the free justification which comes by faith in his blood...the general consent of all that sect is that God...has no sure election, neither yet any certain reprobation, but that every man may elect or reprobate himself by his own free will.[1]

What was it about Anabaptism that made it abhorrent to the reformers?

The Anabaptists were a diverse lot. They ranged from the pacifistic Menno Simons to the mad millennialists of Munster. Almost in wonderment, the reformers spoke of the "marvelous and manifold divisions and bands (of Anabaptists)." What they all held in common was the rejection of infant baptism. This meant that all those who had been baptized as infants were required to be baptized as adults. Hence their name, "Anabaptists," that is, "Rebaptizers." Their rejection of infant baptism was not an incidental matter to the Anabaptists but the chief article of their religion. In a letter to Thomas Muntzer, Conrad Grebel railed on infant baptism as "a senseless, blasphemous abomination, contrary to all Scripture."[2] The very first article of the document that comes closest to being an Anabaptist statement of faith, the Schleitheim Confession of 1527, repudiates infant baptism as "the highest and chief abomination of the pope."[3]

The rejection of infant baptism involved the denial of the covenant, both with regard to the inclusion of the children of believers and with regard to the unity of the Old and New Testaments. It also meant the denial of original sin and total depravity. A leading Anabaptist, Pilgram Marpeck, wrote that it is only when children grow in the knowledge of good and evil, that sin, death, and condemnation come into play.

With one voice, the Anabaptists preached the false gospel of salvation by free will. Such was the place of, and so did they stress, good works in their teaching that they denied, if they did not set aside entirely, justification by faith alone—the heartbeat of the Reformation and the cornerstone of the biblical gospel. The first article of the confession of faith of Anabaptism's leading theologian, Balthasar Hubmaier, was, "Faith alone makes us holy [German: *Fromm*, "pious"] before God."[4] Thus he clearly expressed Anabaptism's radical difference from the Reformation. For the Reformation, the first article of faith is righteousness by faith alone, a righteousness that has nothing to do with man's works but consists of the imputation to him of the obedience of Christ. For Anabaptism, the first article is man's own holiness, a holiness that does not have its source in a preceding justification.

But the Anabaptists had little use for sound doctrine and none for creeds. Their concern was instead the Christian life, good works, spiritual experience, and a holy congregation.

Running strongly through the movement, until the debacle at Munster dampened its ardor, was a revolutionary spirit. Not only did the Anabaptists despise and reject civil government as the epitome of the godlessness of the world, but they also yearned to overturn the entire established order.

Fueling this fire was the dream of establishing the kingdom of heaven here and now. The saints must rule. The "Fifth Monarchy" of Daniel's vision must become an earthly reality through the efforts of the saints.

It should surprise no one that both the *Institutes* of Calvin and the Belgic Confession had as one of their main purposes to disassociate the Reformed churches from Anabaptism.

It is, however, the urgency of the conflict of the Reformed faith with Anabaptism in our day that needs to be sounded and appreciated. If one thinks only of the physical descendants of the Anabaptists, the Hutterites in South Dakota and the Amish in Indiana, he will regard the notion of a conflict as nonsense. But let him consider that the spiritual descendants of the Anabaptists dominate the American religious scene. Non-Roman Catholic religion in America is overwhelmingly Anabaptist. It rejects infant baptism; the covenant; total depravity; justification by faith alone; and sovereign, gracious predestination. Its gospel is salvation by free will and good works. It is anti-doctrinal and anti-confessional. It spurns the unity of the church as manifested in a denomination. It is individualistic; experience-centered; and millennial, dreaming the Anabaptist dream of the thousand-year, carnal reign of Christ on earth.

There is even in some quarters the surfacing of the latent Anabaptist characteristic of revolution. The latter-day Anabaptists are willing to resort to force against the state over their church-schools, over abortion, and over other laws that they judge oppressive and unjust.

These churches call themselves evangelical or fundamentalist. In fact, they are Anabaptist.

The preachers who are the successors of Carlstadt, Muntzer, Grebel, Hutter, and Joris are Billy Graham, Jack Hyles, Jerry Falwell, Ed Dobson, Bill Hybels, and the entire charismatic swarm.

In one of history's ironies, the Anabaptists who once skulked in woods and fields, the outlaws of society, now worship in huge cathedrals and command the attention, and even deference, of the president.

The Reformed churches are wide open to the Anabaptist influence. They eagerly adopt Anabaptist doctrines and ways. In Grand Rapids, Michigan, Reformed people flock to the Anabaptist services at Calvary Church, Resurrection Life Church, and Mars Hill Church. Reformed consistories welcome the popular Anabaptist preachers to their pulpits.

A recent account in a Reformed periodical of a convention of supposedly young Calvinists read like the description of a wilder Anabaptist evangelistic meeting: invitations to children of the covenant to walk the aisle to embrace Jesus for the first time; music calculated to stir the emotions; arms waving in the power of the Spirit; and even a ritual of Christian hugging.[5] And the leaders in the denomination approve. All that remains is to rebaptize as adults, repudiating infant baptism. This is coming.

Is the warning against Anabaptism urgent in our day?

Anabaptism has almost extinguished the light of the Reformed faith rekindled by the Spirit of Christ at the Reformation.

But not quite. And not ever.

There are still confessional Reformed churches that maintain the life-and-death conflict of the Reformation with the Anabaptist radicals. Among them are the Protestant Reformed Churches. This too is an irony of church history. For the beginning of the existence of the Protestant Reformed Churches was that they were cast out of the Christian Reformed Church as "Anabaptist." "*Doopersch*," their adversaries shouted. It was a ridiculous charge. Denial of common grace was supposed to lead to "world-flight." In their response, *Niet Doopersch maar Gereformeerd* (Not Anabaptist but Reformed), Henry Danhof and Herman Hoeksema dismissed the pitiful accusation as mere "mud-slinging."

> "World-flight" is absolutely not our view. Exactly the opposite is our view. We exactly are determined not to go out of the world. It is exactly our intention to abandon not one single area of life. We have exactly called to God's people that it must occupy all of life. Only, we are

determined that this people of the Lord, which is His covenant people, shall not forsake or deny its God in any area of life. In every sphere, that people has been called to live out of grace, out of the one grace, by which it has been implanted into Christ..."World-flight," therefore, is not applicable to us...If by "world" you mean "nature," you see clearly that we do not separate nature and grace, but everywhere want to live out of grace. And if you mean "world" in the evil sense, we do not take to flight from the world, but fight the good fight to the end.[6]

Let it be known that the Protestant ("Anabaptist") Reformed Churches contend as sharply with the Anabaptist churches as they do with Rome. Like Rome, the Anabaptists are false churches. This is the official Reformed judgment upon them in Article 29 of the Belgic Confession.[7]

In this conflict, we renounce the physical means that were once sinfully used against the wretched Anabaptists—drowning, fire, and sword. Those accomplished nothing anyway, except to spread the heresy.

We use the weapon of the word of God, the word of free, sovereign grace in the covenant.

Precisely the same weapon with which we contend with Rome.

Part 3

Doctrines and Issues

10

The Bible, a Divine Book: John Calvin's Doctrine of Holy Scripture

Dale Kuiper

JUST AS CHILDREN OF THE REFORMATION UNDERSTAND that the greatest event between Pentecost and the return of Christ was above all a return to the Scriptures, so Calvinists ought to know what the theologian of the Reformation held those Scriptures to be.

> It was Calvin's *Institutes* which, with its calm, clear, positive exposition of the evangelical faith in the irrefragable authority of Holy Scripture, gave stability to wavering minds, and confidence to sinking hearts, and placed upon the lips of all a brilliant apology in the face of the calumnies of the enemies of the Reformation.[1]

Calvin's view of Scripture is set forth in the first nine chapters of the *Institutes*. It is only after he has laid down the principle of biblical authority that he allows himself and the reader to proceed to a consideration of the doctrines of God, man, Christ, salvation, and the church. In chapters one through five Calvin treats such subjects as the connection between the knowledge of God and the knowledge of ourselves, the nature of the knowledge of God, and what the fall has done to man's knowledge. He stresses in chapter six that the guidance and teaching of Scripture is necessary even to know God rightly as creator. Repeatedly he emphasizes that

"God not only uses mute teachers [creation], but even opens his own sacred mouth; not only proclaims that some god ought to be worshipped, but at the same time pronounces himself to be the Being to whom this worship is due." He reminds us that he is not treating the covenant or salvation in the first nine chapters, but "only showing how we ought to learn from the Scripture, that God, who created the world, may be certainly distinguished from the whole multitude of fictitious deities."[2]

It is clear, therefore, that Calvin taught that the study of creation by science, although more than sufficient to deprive the ingratitude of men of every excuse, was not sufficient to give anything more than confused notions of deity. There is not, in his view, a reciprocal relation between Scripture and scientific findings by which each casts true light upon the other, as the theistic evolutionist holds today. Calvinists must avoid that proud pitfall and confess that Scripture alone gives us the truth regarding creation and the creator.

The Establishment of Scripture's Authority

In chapter seven of *Institutes*, Calvin teaches that unless the authority of Scripture is firmly established, doubts will flourish and there will be a lack of reverence for the word.

> But since we are not favoured with daily oracles from heaven, and since it is only in the Scriptures that the Lord hath been pleased to preserve his truth in perpetual remembrance, it obtains the same complete credit and authority with believers, when they are satisfied of its divine origin, as if they heard the very words pronounced by God himself.[3]

Calvin calls it a "pernicious error" to teach that the Scriptures derive their authority and weight by the suffrages of the church, or that the church decides what reverence is due the Scriptures, and what books comprise the canon.[4]

By quoting Ephesians 2:20, which says that the church is built upon the foundation of the apostles and prophets, Calvin destroys the argument that the Scriptures depend on the church's decisions. If the foundation of the church is Scripture, then Scripture precedes the existence of the church, and the church cannot exist without Scripture. How, then, can she be the judge of them? "Wherefore, when the church receives it, and seals it with her suffrage, she does not authenticate a thing otherwise dubious or controvertible; but knowing it to be the truth of her God, performs a duty of piety, by treating it with immediate veneration."[5]

The enemies of biblical authority like to quote Augustine's line "that he would not believe the Gospel unless he were influenced by the authority of the church."[6] Calvin calls this false and unfair because the context of Augustine's statement is ignored. Augustine, when arguing against the Manichees, writes this only of aliens from the faith who could not be persuaded to believe the gospel as the truth of God unless they saw uniform agreement in the church. For how can the church command the obedience of faith if she herself does not agree on doctrine? Augustine held that the authority of the church was only an introduction to prepare the hearer for the faith of the gospel.

Calvin insists that the principal proof for the authority of the Bible is derived from the character of the Divine Speaker. "The prophets and apostles boast not of their own genius, or any of those talents which conciliate the faith of the hearers; nor do they insist on arguments from reason; but bring forward the sacred name of God, to compel the submission of the whole world." He immediately adds, "The testimony of the Spirit is superior to all reason. For as God alone is a sufficient witness of himself in his own word, so also the word will never gain credit in the hearts of men, till it be confirmed by the internal testimony of the Spirit."[7] What must we think of twenty-first-century Calvinists who wonder at the nature and extent of biblical authority? Why do they appoint committees to study such a question? It is faithless conniving against the fundamental principle of the Reformation.

After calling it an undeniable truth that "they who have been inwardly taught by the Spirit, feel an entire acquiescence in the Scripture, and that it is self-authenticated, carrying with it its own evidence," a grand statement echoed in Article 5 of the Belgic Confession, Calvin is not afraid to place the inability of reason to establish the Bible as the word of God right alongside the reasonableness of faith which believes this is so. "It is such a persuasion, therefore, as requires no reasons; such a knowledge as is supported by the highest reason, in which, indeed, the mind rests with greater security and constancy than in any reasons; it is, finally, such a sentiment as cannot be produced but by a revelation from heaven."[8] This is what every believer experiences in the depths of his heart. This is what Isaiah means when he states, "All the children shall be taught of God" (Isa. 54:13). And this great gift of faith is what distinguishes the elect from the rest of mankind. Only the elect are given to understand the mysteries of God.

Rational Proofs Assist Belief in Scripture

Although faith is necessary to establish the truth and authority of Scripture in one's heart, Calvin concedes that certain rational proofs can help the believer in his confession and defense of biblical doctrine—but only if the foundation of faith has first been laid. "Whilst, on the contrary, when, regarding it in a different point of view from common things, we have once religiously received it in a manner worthy of its excellence, we shall then derive great assistance from things which before were not sufficient to establish the certainty of it in our minds." Calvin has in mind the "order and disposition of the Divine Wisdom dispensed" in Scripture; the "heavenly nature of its doctrine, which never savours of any thing terrestrial"; the "beautiful agreement of all parts with each other"; and the "dignity of the subjects [rather] than the beauties of the language." He believes that

The Bible, a Divine Book

"the force of truth in the sacred Scripture is too powerful to need the assistance of verbal art" and "that the sublime mysteries of the kingdom of heaven [are] communicated, for the most part, in humble and contemptible style."[9]

Nevertheless, the "diction of some of the prophets is neat and elegant, and even splendid; so that they are not inferior in eloquence to the heathen writers. And by such examples the Holy Spirit hath been pleased to show, that he was not deficient in eloquence, though elsewhere he hath used a rude and homely style."[10] Whether biblical language is a sweet flow of words or characterized by rusticity, the inspiration of the Spirit is everywhere in evidence.

Another assisting proof to faith in Scripture is the endurance of the word of God throughout all generations. Himself in awe, Calvin writes,

> For it is not an unimportant consideration, that, since the publication of the Scripture, so many generations of men should have agreed in voluntarily obeying it; and that however Satan, together with the whole world, has endeavored by strange methods to suppress or destroy it, or utterly to erase and obliterate it from the memory of man, yet it has always, like a palm-tree, risen superior to all opposition, and remained invincible."[11]

Calvin ascribes the preserving of Scripture throughout the ages, not to the church or the faithfulness of men, but to the providence of God. This comforting, historical fact is further proof that the Bible is a divine book.

The final proof that can assist our faith in receiving the doctrines of the Bible with confidence is that Scripture has been confirmed by the blood of so many saints.

> Having once received it, they hesitated not, with intrepid boldness, and even with great alacrity, to die in its defence: transmitted to us with such a pledge, how should we not receive it with a firm and unshaken conviction? Is it therefore no small confirmation of the Scripture, that it has been sealed with the blood of so many martyrs?

Calvin closes chapter eight of *Institutes* with the reminder that "the Scripture will then only be effectual to produce the saving knowledge of God, when the certainty of it shall be founded on the internal persuasion of the Holy Spirit. Thus those human testimonies, which contribute to its confirmation will not be useless, if they follow that first and principal proof, as secondary aids to our imbecility."[12]

Claims of Special Revelations Subversive to Piety

Calvin is intolerant of those who pretend not to need the Scripture because they have received special revelations from the Spirit. He calls this attempt to separate word and Spirit ridiculous, puerile, mean, and subversive. "The office of the Spirit, then, which is promised to us, is not to feign new and unheard of revelations, or to coin a new system of doctrine, which would seduce us from the received doctrine of the Gospel, but to seal to our minds the same doctrine which the Gospel delivers."[13] Since the Spirit is the author of Scripture, he cannot by secret revelations be inconsistent with himself. He always testifies to his own truth which he has expressed in Scripture, with the result that "he only displays and exerts his power where the word is received with due reverence and honour."[14] The antidote to the growing mysticism and improper emphasis on the Spirit in our day is the Reformation doctrine of the sufficiency of Holy Scripture.

Calvin sharply limits what can be known from creation to confused notions of deity, denies that the authority of Scripture depends on decisions of the church, warns against rational arguments for biblical inspiration if faith is not first present, and concludes with severe criticism of those who would separate word and Spirit. Extensive quotations from the *Institutes* show this. Is not your appetite whetted to give the *Institutes* a first, or another, careful reading?

11

The Reformation and Biblical Interpretation

Herman Hanko

ONE PART OF THE GREAT HERITAGE OF THE PROTESTANT Reformation, to which we owe so much, is its doctrine of Scripture. Not only did the Reformation return the Scriptures to the church, but the reformers laid down fundamental principles of biblical interpretation that the faithful church has followed to the present. Many, even in Reformed and Presbyterian circles, have abandoned these principles in the interests of accommodation to modem secular trends and scientific discoveries, but the church that is faithful to the word has cherished what the reformers insisted on as the only correct method of biblical interpretation.

Medieval Background

The Roman Catholic Church effectively took the Bible from the people of God. It did this in the firm belief that only the trained, ordained clergy were capable of understanding Scripture. Rome not only considered the Bible to be obscure and difficult to interpret, but also maintained that the people of God do not possess the spiritual ability to understand the Scriptures. Rome, therefore, forbade the

The Sixteenth-Century Reformation of the Church

common people to possess and read God's word and persecuted those who attempted to translate the Scriptures into the common tongue and distribute God's word to God's people. William Tyndale was killed for translating the Scriptures into the English language.

The obscurity of the Scriptures was due, according to Rome, to the fact that Scripture had four levels of interpretation, each of which penetrated deeper into the sacred text, and taken together gave Scripture a four-fold meaning. The literal meaning lay on the surface, but beneath the meaning was also, according to Thomas Aquinas, a figurative, moral, and anagogical or spiritual meaning.[1] To penetrate these different levels of interpretation required someone extremely skilled in biblical interpretation. Such skill was beyond the ability of the majority of the people of God.

According to Roman Catholic teaching, Scripture derived its authority from the church. While this meant many different things, it also meant that only the church possessed the authority to interpret Scripture. What the church said Scripture meant, that was its true meaning.

Thus the Bible was forcibly snatched from the hands of God's people. And so it is today. With the methods of interpretation employed by those who defend women in ecclesiastical office, evolutionism, and homosexuality, the Bible has become a closed book to all but the "experts." It is no wonder that Bible study is on the decline. Who cares to read a book that one cannot understand in its true meaning? Why read God's narrative of creation if the Bible does not mean what it says? Reading the Bible would be an exercise in futility.

The Doctrine of Scripture

With a few minor exceptions, all the reformers of the sixteenth-century Reformation agreed on the doctrine of Scripture. Luther, Zwingli, Knox, Calvin, and all the second-generation reformers held to the truth that Scripture is a unique and God-inspired book.

The whole question of the nature of inspiration was not discussed much by the reformers, chiefly because it was not an issue with Rome. But the reformers firmly held that Scripture in all its parts, even its very words, is the word of God. Calvin writes in his commentary on 2 Timothy 3:16:

> Whoever then wishes to profit in the Scriptures, let him, first of all, lay down this as a settled point, that the Law and the Prophets are not a doctrine delivered according to the will and pleasure of men, but dictated by the Holy Spirit…We owe to the Scripture the same reverence which we owe to God; because it has proceeded from him alone, and has nothing belonging to man mixed with it.[2]

Along with this truth of inspiration, the reformers also believed that Scripture is the sole authority in matters of faith and life. This is the truth, sometimes called "the formal principle of the Reformation," *sola Scriptura*—Scripture alone.

It is sad that this principle is so recklessly abandoned today. Those who support evolutionism use as one of their arguments that the creation clearly demonstrates evolutionism; that the creation is also God's revelation; and that, therefore, we must accept the testimony of creation along with Scripture. Many of those who attempt to promote women in ecclesiastical office openly admit that Scripture is opposed to this notion, but they insist that Scripture must be interpreted in the light of our modern times. Thus Scripture is no longer the sole authority for our faith (in creation) and our life (in the church of Christ).

The Scriptures do not derive their authority from the church, as Rome maintained. The Scriptures are authoritative because they are divinely inspired. They have the authority of God behind them. Thus the Scriptures are self-authenticating; that is, the Scriptures themselves testify of their divine origin and authority. The Belgic Confession, Article 5 has the title "Whence Do the Holy Scriptures Derive Their Dignity and Authority" and it reads,

> We receive all these books, and these only, as holy and canonical, for the regulation, foundation, and confirmation of our faith; believing, without any doubt, all things contained in them, not so much because the Church receives them and approves them as such, but more especially because the Holy Ghost witnesseth in our hearts that they are from God, whereof they carry the evidence in themselves. For the very blind are able to perceive that the things foretold in them are fulfilling.[3]

Thus the Belgic Confession rests the self-authentication of Scripture on the objective testimony of Scripture itself and the subjective testimony of the Spirit in the hearts of the people of God.

The second point of "The Ten Conclusions of Berne" (1528), drawn up under Zwingli's influence, states: "The Church of Christ makes no laws and commandments without the Word of God. Hence human traditions are no more binding on us than as far as they are founded in the Word of God."[4] Luther's stirring appeal to Scripture at the Diet of Worms was a total commitment to the authority of Scripture, although he had come to this position two years earlier at the Leipzig Disputation where he had debated with the Roman theologian John Eck.

Further, the reformers recognized that the authority of Scripture necessarily implied the truth of Scripture's perspicuity. The reformers insisted, contrary to Rome, that Scripture is clear and easy to understand. But Scripture's perspicuity was, in turn, based on the truth that the literal meaning of Scripture is the correct and only meaning. Believers can and do understand the Scriptures, and they can and do make Scripture the rule of canon of their lives. Scripture is clear; Scripture is authoritative.

Rules for Biblical Interpretation: The Grammatico-Historical Method

When Rome spoke of four levels of meaning in Scripture, the fact is that, other than the literal meaning, the three

The Reformation and Biblical Interpretation

deeper levels of meaning were all allegorical. Thus, all Scripture was, according to Rome, basically allegorical and the true meaning could not be determined apart from an allegorizing of the sacred text.

Over against this view, the reformers held to the grammatico-historical method. By this they meant several things.

They meant, first, that Scripture is the record of God's revelation in history, and that a text must be explained in its historical setting. For example, one must understand what the temple meant for Solomon and Israel when it was built in order to understand what God is saying to us in the building of the temple.

Second, Scripture is written in human language and must be interpreted according to the rules of Hebrew and Greek. God wrote Scripture in our language so that we could understand it. God spoke of himself clearly. Calvin compared God's speech to us with the "lisping" of a nursemaid who speaks in a way the child can understand.[5]

Third, by the grammatico-historical method the reformers meant that Scripture is to be taken literally. While this principle cannot be so rigidly applied to Scripture that even figures of speech and symbols are taken literally (as the Anabaptists attempted to explain Scripture), Scripture itself will clearly indicate when it is not to be taken in its literal sense. Luther put it this way: "The Christian reader should make it his first task to seek out the literal sense, as they call it. For it alone is the whole substance of faith and Christian theology; it alone holds its ground in trouble and trial."[6]

Fourth, this literal sense destroys allegory once and for all. Luther had learned the hopelessness of allegory while he was a monk, and he sharply condemned such interpretation as "mere jugglery," "a merry chase," "monkey tricks," and "looney talk."[7]

The reformers did not deny that some Scriptures are more difficult to understand than others, but, as Luther said: "A doubtful and obscure passage must be explained by a clear and certain passage," for "Scripture is its own light. It is a fine thing when Scripture explains itself."[8]

Christ-centered Interpretation

It is, said the reformers, the literal meaning of Scripture that will lead us to Christ. Allegory hides Christ. The literal meaning leads the believer to Christ. "He who would read the Bible," Luther said, "must simply take heed that he does not err, for the Scripture may permit itself to be stretched and led, but let no one lead it according to his own inclinations but let him lead it to the source, that is the cross of Christ. Then he will surely strike the centre."[9]

Christ is the "center" of Scripture, for Scripture reveals to us our salvation and leads us to Christ. "Whatever does not teach Christ is not apostolic, even though St. Peter or St. Paul does the teaching. Again, whatever preaches Christ would be apostolic, even if Judas, Annas, Pilate, and Herod were doing it."[10]

The Spirit Interprets Scripture

Perhaps the most fundamental principle of all is the reformers' insistence that the Holy Spirit alone interprets Scripture.

This means two things.

It means, first, that Scripture interprets Scripture. The reformers insisted that this principle, sometimes called the "analogy of faith," was not merely a principle of convenience. By it they meant that Scripture is the Spirit's book, for it is inspired by the Spirit as a unity; and the Spirit uses his own writings in one place to explain his writings in another place.

Second, and equally important, the Spirit is the interpreter of Scripture in the hearts of the people of God. Reason cannot explain Scripture, for the man who relies upon reason is an unbeliever whose mind is darkened. To him Scripture is a "closed book." Scripture, Luther said, "is foreign and strange to reason, and particularly to the worldly-wise. No man can accept it unless his heart has been touched and opened by the Holy Spirit."[11] The Holy Spirit alone can open the Scriptures because the Holy Spirit gives faith by which we lay hold on Christ taught us in God's word.

Thus the interpreter of Scripture is the man who comes to Scripture in humility, seeking to be taught by the Holy Spirit that he may take Christ as his all-sufficient Savior.

Would that these towering principles of the Reformation were still the confession of the church!

12

"Far Brighter Even Than the Sun"

David J. Engelsma

It is well known that Martin Luther's great work, *The Bondage of the Will*, sets forth the Reformation's central doctrine of salvation by the sovereign grace of God alone. The introduction to J. I. Packer's and O. R. Johnston's translation of *The Bondage of the Will* calls the book "the greatest piece of theological writing that ever came from Luther's pen." It quotes the Reformation scholar E. Gordon Rupp as approving the description of *The Bondage of the Will* as "the finest and most powerful Soli Deo Gloria to be sung in the whole period of the Reformation." Accurately, it identifies its message as the heart of the theology of all the reformers: "the sinner's entire salvation is by free and sovereign grace only."[1]

What is not so well known is that this grand work on the central message of the gospel also puts forward a splendid defense of Holy Scripture as the source and standard of the gospel. This defense focuses on the clarity, or perspicuity, of Scripture. Clarity is a quality of Scripture that is somewhat overlooked in the struggle of the Reformed church today to maintain a sound doctrine of Scripture. To the mind of Luther, clarity is basic to a sound doctrine of Scripture and to the functioning of Scripture as the word of God in the church. Denial of Scripture's clarity is the destruction of the doctrine of Scripture.

"Far Brighter Even Than the Sun"

The defense of Scripture's clarity is no incidental aspect of *The Bondage of the Will*. With this, Luther begins. It is a recurring theme in the book, undergirding the message of sovereign grace. *The Bondage of the Will* presents the two great truths of the Reformation, sovereign grace and the authority of Scripture, in their unity.

The reason for Luther's consideration of the clarity of Scripture lay in the book that occasioned his writing *The Bondage of the Will*. This was Erasmus' defense of free will, *A Diatribe concerning Free Will*. In his attack on Luther's teaching that the will of fallen man is enslaved to sin, Erasmus suggests that Scripture is not clear on the issue of the bound or free will:

> If you turn your eyes to Scripture, both sides claim it as their own. Furthermore, our controversy is not merely over Scripture (which is somewhat deficient in clarity at present), but over the precise meaning of Scripture; and here not the numbers, learning and distinction on the one side, much less the paucity, ignorance and lack of distinction on the other, can advance either cause.[2]

The implication, Luther notes, is that "the matter is therefore left in doubt."[3]

Luther regards Erasmus' opinion that Scripture is obscure as grave error. The result of this notion in the church will be that the views of men replace the word of God:

> No more disastrous words could be spoken; for by this means ungodly men have exalted themselves above the Scriptures and done what they liked, till the Scriptures were completely trodden down and we could believe and teach nothing but maniacs' dreams. In a word, that dictum is no mere human invention; it is poison sent into the world by the inconceivably malevolent prince of all the devils himself![4]

It was exactly this doubt concerning Scripture's clarity that enabled the pope to subdue the church, and Scripture, to himself:

83

> On the same account I have thus far hounded the Pope, in whose kingdom nothing is more commonly said or more widely accepted than this dictum: "the Scriptures are obscure and equivocal; we must seek the interpreting Spirit from the apostolic see of Rome!"[5]

Expressing a conviction that would become the foundation of the Reformation, Luther asserts that the Scriptures are clear—"far brighter even than the sun":

> It should be settled as fundamental, and most firmly fixed in the minds of Christians, that the Holy Scriptures are a spiritual light far brighter even than the sun, especially in what relates to salvation and all essential matters.[6]

The entire Scripture is clear. Scripture is clear in its totality. The whole of it is light, not darkness. The difficult passages are clarified by the other passages.

The clarity of Scripture is twofold: internal and external. The internal clarity is the enlightening of the Holy Spirit, which gives understanding of all the teachings of the Scriptures. Every believer has this enlightening. The external clarity is the inherent perfection of Scripture itself. The Holy Book is not obscure or ambiguous. Rather, its meaning is plain.[7]

Two important qualifications attach to the external clarity of Scripture. The first is that Scripture is clear to believers through the preaching of Scripture: "All that is in the Scripture is *through the Word* brought forth into the clearest light."[8] This is intriguing. Luther personally and the Reformation generally refused to separate Scripture from the preaching of Scripture. Scripture is light, but it shines through faithful preaching, not otherwise.

The second qualification attaching to the external clarity is that Scripture must be interpreted in its simple, natural sense. Clarity rejects, indeed abominates, the allegorizing methods of interpretation. Luther sharply criticizes Origen and Jerome for their "pestilent practice of paying no heed to the simple sense of Scripture."[9]

"Far Brighter Even Than the Sun"

What proof is there that Scripture is clear? This is an urgent question especially because Erasmus had raised the argument that many men of superior ability did not understand Scripture on the issue of the bound will as Luther explained it. Does this not prove that Scripture is obscure? The proof of Scripture's clarity, says Luther, is the testimony of Scripture itself. Scripture claims to be clear. Luther cites and explains Deuteronomy 17:8; Psalm 19:8; Psalm 119:105, 130; Isaiah 8:20; Malachi 2:7; 2 Corinthians 3, 4; and 2 Peter 1:19. Luther readily acknowledges that this way of proving Scripture's clarity amounts to "arguing in a circle." One appeals to Scripture to prove that one can appeal to Scripture. But this is the "circle" of the Reformation faith that Scripture is the word of God.

The reason that many of superior ability have not understood Scripture rightly is their own natural, sinful blindness. Indeed, Erasmus himself, the most learned scholar in Christendom, denies Scripture's clear teaching of the bound will because he is a blind man standing in the bright rays of the "external clarity" of Scripture:

> The Diatribe [of Erasmus, that is, Erasmus himself] and its beloved Sophists, standing open-eyed under the bright light of Luke's words and of clear fact, continue in blindness; such is their lack of care in reading and marking the Scriptures. And then they have to brand them "obscure and ambiguous"![10]

The church must know the clarity of Scripture for two main reasons. The first is eminently practical: only then will Christians read Scripture. What fool will bother to study and to hear preached an obscure book? By suggesting that Scripture is obscure, Erasmus "well-nigh frightened us off reading the Bible altogether—though Bible-reading is something to which Christ and the Apostles urgently exhort us."[11] In Erasmus' charge that "in Scripture some things are recondite and all is not plain," Luther sees the horns and hooves of Satan:

> Satan has used these unsubstantial spectres to scare men off reading the sacred text, and to destroy all sense of its value, so as to ensure that his own brand of poisonous philosophy reigns supreme in the church.[12]

The second reason that the church must be convinced of Scripture's clarity is that only then will the church make "assertions." Concern that the church make "assertions" is the heart of Luther's defense of the clarity of Scripture in *The Bondage of the Will*. By "assertions," Luther means firm confessions of all the teachings of Scripture. Included is the rejection of all errors.

> By "assertion" I mean staunchly holding your ground, stating your position, confessing it, defending it and persevering in it unvanquished.[13]

So uncompromising is the asserting Christian that he is ready "to die for what [he] confess[es] and assert[s]."[14]

Luther takes up this matter of asserting at the outset of *The Bondage of the Will* because Erasmus had disparaged assertions. Erasmus found no satisfaction in assertions, preferring "an undogmatic temper to any other."[15] Erasmus of Rotterdam, uncharacteristic Dutchman, was the compromiser, ready to give up doctrine for peace. This marked him, as far as Luther was concerned, as no genuine Christian, for "to take no pleasure in assertions is not the mark of a Christian heart; indeed, one must delight in assertions to be a Christian at all." Asserting is the essence of Christianity: "Take away assertions, and you take away Christianity."[16]

The true church of Christ is an asserting church. Every real Christian is an asserting Christian. Particularly, every true church and every real Christian assert the bondage of the will of the natural man and the salvation of every sinner by sovereign grace alone.

The alternative is doubt and uncertainty about the doctrines of the Bible, that is, skepticism. This is impossible, in Luther's glorious statement, because "the Holy Spirit is no

Sceptic, and the things He has written in our hearts are not doubts or opinions, but assertions— surer and more certain than sense and life itself."[17]

The church must assert, but she can assert only if Scripture is clear, since she asserts "what has been delivered to us from above in the Sacred Scriptures."[18]

How evident it is that Protestant churches and professing Protestant Christians at the beginning of the twenty-first century have lost the faith that Scripture is clear.

They cannot assert!

They cannot assert the bondage of the will. They cannot assert biblical creation. They cannot assert the cessation of the extraordinary gifts of the Spirit. They cannot assert the exclusion of women from the government of the church. They cannot assert the wickedness of divorce except in the case of fornication. They cannot assert the lawfulness of sex only within the lifelong bond of marriage between a man and a woman.

They can only assert that there ought not be assertions in the church.

Their synodical decisions and personal testimonies run like this: "Scripture does not make clear, and we cannot decide with certainty…"

What use, we ask, is a Scripture that is unclear on every issue? Whatever could have been the motivation of an otherwise wise God to give us more obscurity in our already sufficient darkness of uncertainty?

But, of course, to propose obscurity as an attribute of Scripture is to open up the way of every error into the church. Pleading uncertainty and appealing to Scripture's obscurity, Desiderius Erasmus advocated free will and opposed the gospel of salvation by the grace of God.

The need of the hour is that churches and Christians assert. They must assert every doctrine of Scripture. They must especially assert the doctrine of the bound will.

They must assert, but they also can and will assert.

For the Scriptures are "a spiritual light far brighter even than the sun."

13

Luther on Preaching

Steven Key

Martin Luther's influence on preaching is well worth considering. The Reformation took root, after all, by the restoration of faithful preaching, with Luther and the other reformers leading the way.

Although it would be an overstatement to say that preaching had been entirely lost prior to the Reformation, it is true that there were very few faithful preachers left in the church, and preaching itself had certainly fallen on hard times. The element of proclamation, the "thus saith the Lord" that is the heart of all true preaching, was all but lost. For that reason one of the most important contributions of Luther to the church was his emphasis on preaching.

Luther himself gives us a view of what preaching commonly involved in his day, openly ridiculing and scorning that which passed for preaching by the unfaithful pastors in the church of his day. The sermons were superficial, often including fables or stories, as well as a mixture of pagan philosophy. Moreover, these "sermons" were often told in a vulgar or comical way, in order to amuse the people. Christ was forgotten. The Scriptures were neglected.

"Oh, we have had blind preachers for a long time; they have been totally blind themselves and leaders of the blind, as the gospel says; they have left the gospel and followed their own ideas and preferred the work of men to the work of God."[1]

Never one to mince words, Luther spoke sharply of unfaithful preachers:

> These are the lazy and worthless preachers who do not tell the princes and lords their sins. In some cases they do not notice the sins. They lie down and snore in their office and do nothing that pertains to it except that, like swine, they take up the room where good preachers should stand.[2]

Over against that corruption of preaching, Luther fervently called for biblical, expository preaching. "It was Luther who rediscovered both the form and the substance of this preaching...For him preaching was the veritable Word of God Himself, and, as such, occupied the central position in the Church."[3] Indeed, the emphasis on preaching the gospel developed into one of the chief marks of the churches of the Reformation and, as Luther never tired of pointing out, gave purpose as well as authority to their existence.

Preaching with Substance

Martin Luther understood that faithful preaching must have substance. That substance is the truth of the gospel, the faithful exposition of Holy Scripture.

A. Skevington Wood summarizes Luther's preaching as follows:

> The salient feature of Luther's preaching was its biblical content and reference. It was subject to Scripture throughout. Luther submitted to a rigorous discipline. He was bound by the Word. His preaching was never merely topical. He could never turn a text into a pretext. "I take pains to treat a verse, to stick to it," he explained, "and so to instruct the people that they can say, 'That is what the sermon was about.'" His preaching was never a movement from men to the text: it was always a movement from the text to men. The matter never

determined the text: the text always determined the matter. He was not in the habit of treating subjects or issues, but doctrines. But when he did so, he invariably followed a prescribed Scripture passage step by step. He considered one of the major qualifications of the preacher to be familiarity with the Word.[4]

Luther taught clearly the centrality of the word. Faith is nothing else but adherence to the word of God. It is this word which breaks down the sinner by the law and which raises up the believer in the gospel.

His high esteem for the word of God explains why Luther also attempted to preach systematically through the Scriptures, preaching series of sermons from both Old and New Testaments.

Because of that biblical emphasis on the primacy of the word and the centrality of preaching, Luther had no place for the false mysticism that sets aside the word of God for inner feelings. "Away with our schismatics, who spurn the Word while they sit in corners waiting for the Spirit's revelation, but apart from the voice of the Word!"[5]

It must be noted in this connection that Luther spoke of preaching in terms of "the voice." He said, "Take note: The beginning of all spiritual knowledge is this *voice of one crying*, as also Paul says, Romans 10:14: 'How are they to believe ... without a preacher?'"[6]

Preaching with Authority

Luther taught clearly that preaching that is faithful and true comes with the authority of "the voice."

This thought reflected Luther's high view of the office. The minister is sent by God and enters the office of God. "Thus St. Paul is confident (2 Cor. 13:3) that he is speaking not his own word, but the Word of the Lord Christ. Thus we, too, can say that He has put it into our mouth."[7]

That truth was important to Luther, too, in the face of all the opposition that darkened his pathway. It was a truth he consistently proclaimed.

In his treatment of Psalm 2, speaking of the office of Christ as Teacher who declares God's decree, Luther explained that the Holy Spirit so teaches us

> that God does everything through the Son. For when the Son preaches the Law, the Father Himself, who is in the Son or one with the Son, preaches. And when we preach about this same decree, Christ Himself preaches, as He says: 'He who hears you hears Me' (Luke 10:16).[8]

The preacher, therefore, is the mouthpiece of God, the instrument through which Christ and God himself speaks.

> We both, pastor and listener, are only pupils; there is only this difference, that God is speaking to you through me. That is the glorious power of the divine Word, through which God Himself deals with us and speaks to us, and in which we hear God Himself.[9]

Commenting on John 14:10, Luther writes, "It is not we who are speaking; it is Christ and God Himself. Hence, when you hear this sermon, you are hearing God Himself. On the other hand, if you despise this sermon, you are despising, not us but God Himself."[10]

Preaching and the Work of the Spirit

Because Christ speaks by the preaching of the gospel, preaching is powerful and effective in accomplishing the purpose whereunto God sends it.

So Luther calls attention in his writings to the place of the Holy Spirit in preaching. Christ works this powerful word by his Holy Spirit. It is through the words of preachers that the Holy Spirit works, convicting the world of sin and establishing the faith of God's elect through the effectual and irresistible call.

The Holy Spirit of Christ gives the preaching its power. Christ draws men to himself through the word alone, rescuing his people from the power of sin and death and giving them freedom, righteousness, and life.

> This great and marvelous thing is accomplished entirely through the office of preaching the Gospel. Viewed superficially, this looks like a trifling thing, without any power, like any ordinary man's speech and word. But when such preaching is heard, His invisible, divine power is at work in the hearts of men through the Holy Spirit. Therefore St. Paul calls the Gospel "a power of God for salvation to everyone who has faith" (Rom. 1:16).[11]

Clearly, preachers are but instruments in God's hands. "What shall we do? We can deplore the blindness and obstinacy of people, but we cannot bring about a change for the better."[12] Only when Christ himself speaks by his Holy Spirit is the preaching powerful to change and bring salvation.

"Neither I nor anyone else can ever preach the Word adequately; the Holy Spirit alone must utter and preach it."[13] For it is the Spirit who works by the word. When through the outward preaching of the word and the inward witness of the Holy Spirit, faith is created, then that which is promised in the gospel becomes effective for the believer.

"Accordingly, it is a Word of power and grace when it infuses the Spirit at the same time that it strikes the ears. But if it does not infuse the Spirit, then he who hears does not differ at all from one who is deaf."[14]

Hearing the Preaching

Not overlooked by Luther was the calling of all who hear the preaching to examine that preaching, to see whether it be faithful to the Holy Scriptures. "Hence this is the touchstone by which all doctrine is to be judged. One must take care and see whether it is the same doctrine that was published in Zion through the apostles." It is such preaching that is used by God as the powerful, saving voice of Christ. "For this alone, as has been said, is the true doctrine, bestowing upon men a right and certain understanding, comfort of heart, and salvation."[15]

Along these lines, Luther faces squarely the question of whether or not Christ speaks through a preacher just because the man occupies the office.

> To begin with, we must know that those who are sent speak the Word of God provided that they adhere to their office and administer it as they received it. In that event, they surely speak the Word of God...A king's ambassador or emissary discharges his duty when he abides by his master's order and instruction. If he fails in this, the king has him beheaded.[16]

When a minister, therefore, faithfully preaches the word of God, Christ is pleased to speak through him by his Holy Spirit; if not, then these words apply to that preacher: "Beware of false prophets!" We must neither speak nor hear anything but the word of God.

For that reason the gospel must be heard and preached. Preaching not only has substance, but also it has very specific content. Luther insists, "The preacher's first message is to teach penitence, removing offenses, proclaim the Law, humiliate and terrify the sinners."[17] Our sin must be exposed by the preaching of the gospel. Concerning the book of Romans, he says,

> The sum and substance of this letter is: to pull down, to pluck up, and to destroy all wisdom and righteousness of the flesh...no matter how heartily and sincerely they may be practiced, and to implant, establish, and make large the reality of sin...For God does not want to save us by our own but by an extraneous righteousness which does not originate in ourselves but comes to us from heaven.[18]

The necessity of preaching man's depravity is found in the fact that grace is given to the humble. Christ came not to save the righteous, but to bring sinners to repentance (Luke 5:32). So Luther says, "They cannot be humble who do not recognize that they are damnable whose sin smells to high heaven...Yearning for grace wells up when recognition of sin has arisen. A sick person seeks the physician when he recognizes the seriousness of his illness."[19]

And because God's people have a continual struggle with their sinful flesh, preaching must be antithetical. It must be preaching that not only sounds the silver trumpet of salvation, but also sounds the horn which exposes and reproves the old man of sin and calls to repentance.

As Luther recognized and experienced, it takes boldness in preaching to serve as Christ's ambassador. But the preacher cannot stop with merely preaching sin, for that would amount to wounding and not binding up, smiting and not healing. "Therefore we must also preach the word of grace and the promise of forgiveness by which faith is taught and aroused."[20]

The focus of all preaching must be Christ. The only content of its message is about him. "This is the gist of your preaching: *Behold your God!* 'Promote God alone, His mercy and grace. Preach Me alone.'"[21]

Soli Deo Gloria was the motto of Luther, therefore, no less than of Calvin. The sovereignty of God occupied a prominent place in all Luther's preaching, for his was indeed gospel preaching. From him also came forth the cry of the Reformation, "Let God be God!" In his words, "The gospel proclaims nothing else but salvation by grace, given to man without any works and merits whatsoever. Natural man cannot abide, hear, or see the gospel. Nor does it enter into the hypocrites, for it casts out their works, declaring that they are nothing and not pleasing to God."[22]

God alone works his wonderwork of grace in saving us. For in Christ alone rests all our salvation. The gospel is preached with the purpose of consoling with grace those who are contrite of heart.

Martin Luther also viewed the importance of preaching in the light of its positive fruits. In opposition to the errors of legalism, he recognized that the Christian life must be a life of thankfulness to God and therefore a conscious laying hold of the gospel of a gracious salvation. Thankful lives follow from faithful preaching.

Luther's approach to preaching is the one that would later be outlined in the Heidelberg Catechism. This is the way of true comfort, wrought by the Spirit through the preaching.

"Thus it is not the stones, the construction, and the gorgeous silver and gold that make a church beautiful and holy; it is the Word of God and sound preaching."[23] And this is preaching in which God is glorified.

Such preaching is God's greatest blessing for his church. "Therefore let those who have the pure Word learn to receive it and to give thanks to the Lord for it, and let them seek the Lord while He may be found."[24] May we, the children of the Reformation, humble ourselves and thank God for faithful preaching. God will surely require that we give an account of our preaching and hearing.

14

Luther, Erasmus, and the Bondage of the Will

Russell Dykstra

Certainly the single best-known work of Martin Luther is *The Bondage of the Will*. This masterpiece deserves the honorable position it holds not only in the body of Luther's works, but also in the writings of all the reformers. It sets forth the truth of God's sovereignty in salvation, eliminating any possibility that man contributes to his own salvation. This is the heart of Luther's theology. This is the heart of the great Reformation. And this is the heart of the Reformed truth still today.

That *The Bondage of the Will* should be written is obviously due to the sovereign providence of God. Early on in the conflict Luther came to the conviction that Rome's teaching on man's will was wrong, and he set forth his views in brief. Already at the Heidelberg Disputation in 1518, Luther affirmed that "since the fall of Adam, or after actual sin, free will exists only in name, and when it does what it can it commits sin." This was one of the forty-one articles condemned by Pope Leo X in 1520. In response, Luther wrote *An Assertion of all the Articles of Martin Luther Condemned by the Latest Bull of Leo X*.[1] In this work Luther is even stronger. He writes,

> Wherefore it is needful to retract this article. For I was wrong in saying that free choice before grace is a reality only in name. I should have said simply: "free choice is in reality a fiction, or a name without reality." For no one has it in his own power to think a good or bad thought, but everything (as Wyclif's article condemned at Constance rightly teaches) happens by absolute necessity.[2]

So it might have remained, were it not for God who sovereignly directed the events of the Reformation and forced Luther to develop this truth more fully and explicitly. The means God used to bring this about was primarily one man, namely, Desiderius Erasmus of Rotterdam. Erasmus was an older contemporary of Luther who is sometimes wrongly associated with the Reformation. He was a world-renowned Renaissance scholar whom God used in various ways to serve the cause of the Reformation. Erasmus prepared a scholarly Greek text of the New Testament which was widely used by the reformers. He was vociferous in his criticism of the immorality and ignorance of the clergy of his day. He was a man of high reputation, very much interested in the church being reformed morally, and to that end he promoted education and scholarship. When Luther's works spread like wildfire across Europe, the world watched intently to see whether Erasmus would throw his support to Luther's cause.

Luther and Erasmus were acquainted with each other before the conflict. Half a year before he posted the Ninety-five Theses in Wittenberg, Luther wrote in a personal letter:

> I am at present reading our Erasmus, but my heart recoils more and more from him. But one thing I admire is, that he constantly and learnedly accuses not only the monks, but the priests, of a lazy, deep-rooted ignorance...Only, I fear he does not spread Christ and God's grace sufficiently abroad, of which he knows very little. The human is to him of more importance than the divine.[3]

And, in a portent of what was to come, he added, "Those who ascribe something to man's freedom of will regard those things differently from those who know only God's free grace."

Yet Luther coveted the support of Erasmus for his cause and wrote a flattering letter to Erasmus in 1519, obviously hoping to establish some relationship with the elder scholar. Erasmus' reply to Luther was cordial. He began, "Greetings, dearest brother in Christ. Your letter gave me great pleasure: it displayed the brilliance of your mind and breathed the spirit of a Christian." However, if Luther was hoping that Erasmus would commit himself to Luther's cause, he would be disappointed. Erasmus stated to Luther that he kept himself "uncommitted, so far as I can, in hopes of being able to do more for the revival of good literature."[4]

It would become increasingly evident that Erasmus and Luther were committed to two different, even antagonistic, causes. The decisive issue would be the doctrine at the heart of the Reformation—the doctrine of sovereign grace. The debate arose in connection with Luther's rejection of a free will in fallen man. Erasmus reacted against that in 1524 with a work entitled *A Diatribe concerning Free Will* in which he defended the ability of fallen man to will the good, rejecting Luther's position.[5] Luther's wrote his classic work, *The Bondage of the Will*, against Erasmus. Erasmus, on his part, was furious and turned against Luther and the Reformation completely.

There is value in examining the arguments that Erasmus used to defend the view of a free will in man. They are relevant, first, because *The Bondage of the Will* was a painstaking refutation of Erasmus' work. Second, Erasmus' work is a good representation of the theology of the Roman Catholic Church against which Luther battled. Third, Erasmus' arguments are significant also because they have been pressed into service by Arminians of every stripe and are used even to the present day.

Even the tone of Erasmus' work on the free will of man is one adopted by enemies of sovereign grace throughout history. He wishes to "pursue the matter without recrimination"; he divulges that he has "an inner temperamental horror of fighting."[6] In fact, he does not like to make assertions of what is correct, preferring rather that merely a discussion be held on the topic.

Concerning Scripture, Erasmus maintains that "there are some secret places in the Holy Scriptures into which God has not wished us to penetrate more deeply." In fact, he is convinced that we ought not "through irreverent inquisitiveness rush into those things which are hidden, not to say, superfluous," among which matters is "whether our will accomplishes anything in things pertaining to eternal salvation."[7]

Erasmus craftily uses several devices to give the appearance of being in the right. He avows his own commitment to the authority of Scripture but maintains that the issue is only the proper *interpretation* of Scripture. He condemns Luther by association, putting Luther's views in the same camp as those previously condemned by the church—the heretical Manichaeans and the pre-reformer John Wycliffe. He calls as witnesses nearly all the ancient church fathers, as well as the medieval scholars, because they had used the term free will. But he fails to distinguish between those fathers who were discussing freedom of choice in things natural (what to wear or eat) versus those who were discussing spiritual choices (to sin or do good).

His basic arguments for the free will of fallen man have a familiar ring for anyone who knows the arguments of the enemies of sovereign grace.

Erasmus insists that the fact that God commands something implies that man has the ability to obey the commands. Since God *commands* men to repent, to turn to him, it must be that man *can* will to do it. He treats divine promises that are in a conditional form in the same way.

Related to the above, Erasmus maintains that God is unjust and cruel if he punishes sinners who could not will to love and obey God. Since God cannot be cruel or unjust, Erasmus deduces that fallen man must have free will. In that connection, he teaches that God's predestination is based on foreknowledge—God foreknew who would rebel and who would obey, and on that basis made his choice.

Erasmus denies that natural man can only do evil. Even the pagans, he avers, do good.

Erasmus maintains the semi-Pelagian position that natural man's will is weak, but not powerless. Man's will needs grace to accomplish the good. He distinguishes several kinds of grace supposedly given to man to assist him. According to Erasmus, the reason why Scripture sometimes speaks of the whole work of salvation belonging to God is not to teach that man actually does nothing, but only "to avoid a dangerous arrogance" in man.[8]

Yet perhaps the most important element in Erasmus' apology for free will is that man must merit something with God. Repeatedly he returns to this. He writes, "How is it that we hear so much of reward if there is no such thing as merit?"[9] That was the bedrock on which the whole Romish system was built—man can merit with God. And did Luther know it!

In his conclusion, Erasmus offers a compromise position to Luther. Erasmus is willing to reduce the contribution of man's will to the absolute minimum. He writes:

> For in my opinion free choice could have been so established as to avoid that confidence in our merits and the other dangers which Luther avoids...On this more accommodating view, it is implied that a man owes all his salvation to divine grace, since the power of free choice is exceedingly trivial in this regard and this very thing which it can do is a work of the grace of God who first created free choice and then freed it and healed it.[10]

So far Erasmus, spiritual descendant of Pelagius, forerunner of Arminius.

Luther wrote his work *The Bondage of the Will* in answer to this brilliant scholar and defender of free will. The matter of man's will was the crucial issue in Luther's mind. He praised Erasmus because he alone among Luther's opponents had recognized that the doctrine of free will was "the grand turning point of the cause." Luther wrote, "You, and you alone saw, what was the grand hinge upon which the whole turned."[11]

How, then, does Luther answer this renowned scholar? In a word, Luther devastates Erasmus' arguments.

To begin with, Luther contemns Erasmus' effort, so much so that he considered not even answering it. Writes Luther, "On so great a subject, you say nothing but what has been said before: therefore, you say less about, and attribute more unto 'Free-will,' than the Sophists have hitherto said and attributed." Luther contends that all these arguments have often been refuted. He adds, "I greatly feel for you for having defiled your most beautiful and ingenious language with such vile trash."[12]

As to the dispute itself, Luther addresses Erasmus' desire that these discussions ought to be conducted without fighting. Luther points out that this is not the way of the history of the church or of the spread of the gospel:

> The world and its god cannot and will not bear the Word of the true God: and the true God cannot and will not keep silence. While, therefore, these two Gods are at war with each other, what can there be else in the whole world, but tumult?... Therefore, to wish to silence these tumults, is nothing else, than to wish to hinder the Word of God, and to take it out of the way... And as to myself, if I did not see these tumults, I should say the Word of God was not in the world.[13]

Luther identifies the central issue and its unspeakable importance. It is essential, he writes, "for a Christian to know, whether or not the will does any thing in those things which pertain unto Salvation. Nay, let me tell you, this is the very hinge upon which our discussion turns." If anyone remains unconvinced that the issue is of great importance for the Christian faith, Luther adds here:

> But if I know not the distinction between our working and the power of God, I know not God Himself. And if I know not God, I cannot worship Him, praise Him, give Him thanks, nor serve Him; for I shall not know how much I ought to ascribe unto myself, and how much unto God.[14]

As to the term "free-will," Luther prefers that the term

never be used, because it deceives people with "the most destructive mockery." It implies that men have the power of free choice in the matter of salvation, when the opposite is true. If the term must be used, Luther would have all to remember that man has,

> as to his goods and possessions the right of using, acting, and omitting, according to his "Free-will"; although, at the same time, that same "Free-will" is overruled by the Free-will of God alone, just as He pleases: but that, God-ward, or in things which pertain unto salvation or damnation, he has no "Free-will," but is a captive, slave, and servant, either to the will of God, or to the will of Satan.[15]

Luther answers the charge that he is opposed by the church of all ages, which would mean, if Luther is correct, that God allowed his church to be in error for centuries. First of all, Luther asserts that Augustine is very much in his corner, a fact that Luther demonstrates repeatedly. Second, he points out that the church, externally considered, from Israel to Luther's day, often did err. Yet, he insists that the church of God and the members are hidden, and that God was pleased to preserve his saints even through those times. The calling, therefore, is to try the spirits. This every Christian can and must do because he has the Spirit of God, and the Scriptures are clear. Luther demonstrates this by quoting copiously from Scripture itself. He asks rhetorically, "If the Scripture be obscure or ambiguous, what need was there for its being sent down from heaven?" Then he turns the argument back on Erasmus: "And why do you also, Erasmus, prescribe to us a form of Christianity, if the Scriptures be obscure to you!"[16]

It is worth noting that Luther demands logical consistency in the formulation of doctrine. He shreds Erasmus' arguments by exposing the contradictions found throughout. He notes that Erasmus' definition of free will is hopelessly vague and thus open to various interpretations. Erasmus claims that man has a will able to choose the good without grace, and in other places maintains that man can will nothing good without the grace of God. Writes Luther, "Hence then, Erasmus, outstripping all others, has two 'Free-wills'; and they, militating against each other!"[17]

What then of the many conditional statements in Scripture adduced by Erasmus—"If thou wilt hear" or "if thou wilt do"? Do these prove that man has a free will to do or to hear? Or is it so, that by these God mocks man, because man cannot obey them anyway? Luther rejects both those conclusions. He writes, "Why is this not rather drawn as a conclusion—therefore, God tries us, that by His law He might bring us to a knowledge of our impotency, if we be His friends; or, He thereby righteously and deservedly insults and derides us, if we be His proud enemies."[18]

Similarly, Luther refutes the Pelagian error that the various commands of God imply that man has the ability to keep them.

> And this is the place, where I take occasion to enforce this my general reply:—that man, by the words of the law, is admonished and taught what *he ought to do*, not what *he can do*: that is, that he is brought to know his sin, but not to believe that he has any strength in himself. Wherefore, friend Erasmus, as often as you throw in my teeth the words of the law, so often I throw in yours that of Paul, "By the law is the knowledge of sin,"—not of the power of the will. Heap together, therefore, out of the large Concordances all the imperative words into one chaos, provided that, they be not words of the promise but of the requirement of the law only, and I will immediately declare, that by them is always shewn what men *ought to do*, not what they *can do*, or *do do*.[19]

Furthermore, Luther takes pains to show that Erasmus proves too much. If all these conditional sentences and commands indicate that man can *will* to do what God enjoins, it necessarily follows that the same statements prove that man can actually do what God commands. Repeatedly Luther reminds Erasmus of the necessary implications—there is no need for the Spirit or grace of God to work in man. He can keep the commandments; he can save himself. Indeed, there is no need even of Christ or the cross.

Luther is quick to remind Erasmus that the Scriptures present a very different picture, namely, "a man, who is not only bound, miserable, captive, sick, and dead, but who, by the operation of his lord, Satan, to his other miseries, adds that of blindness: so that he believes he is free, happy, at liberty, powerful, whole, and alive."[20]

The question naturally arises, why then do some believe and obey, and others do not, if all men are in bondage. Luther asserts that this is due to the "SECRET AND TO BE FEARED WILL OF GOD, who, according to His own counsel, ordains whom, and such as, He will to be receivers and partakers of the preached and offered mercy."[21] Even the conditional sentences must be understood in light of predestination. Writes Luther,

> "If thou wilt": that is, if thou be such with God, that he shall deign to give thee this will to keep the commandments, thou shalt be saved. According to which manner of speaking, it is given us to understand both truths—that we can do nothing ourselves; and that, if we do any thing, God works that in us.[22]

Luther takes on the giant—the issue of merit. Luther rejects Erasmus' conclusion that the promises of reward prove that the will can merit with God. He reminds Erasmus that the promises are exactly that—gracious promises of what God will do. In addition, he points out that these are promises to God's people, and the promise is not to the supposed free will of fallen man, but to men "raised above 'Free-will' in grace, and justified."[23] As far as anyone's ever being worthy of reward, that is impossible, Luther maintains.

> For if "Free-will" cannot of itself will good, but wills good by grace alone, (for we are speaking of "Free-will" apart from grace and inquiring into the power which properly belongs to each) who does not see, that that good will, merit, and reward, belong to grace alone.[24]

Luther points out yet another flaw in Erasmus' argument. He draws the logical consequence that if it be allowed that man can by free will choose the good, then God is "robbed of His power and wisdom to elect." He adds:

> Nay, we shall at length come to this: that men may be saved and damned without God's knowing anything at all about it; as not having determined by certain election who should be saved and who should be damned; but having set before all men in general His hardening goodness and long-suffering, and His mercy shewing correction and punishment, and left them to choose for themselves whether they would be saved or damned.[25]

Not only so, but Luther points to other truths that absolutely rule out the possibility of a free will in man, namely, God's sovereignty and his foreknowledge. God is omnipotent, otherwise "He would be a ridiculous God." At the same time, God "knows and foreknows all things, and neither can err nor be deceived." The "inevitable consequence" is that there is no such thing as a free will. Luther recognizes that this is an offense to man, who charges "that the God, who is set forth as being so full of mercy and goodness, should, of His mere will, leave men, harden them, and damn them, as though He delighted in the sins, and in the great and eternal torments of the miserable."[26] Luther's response to the charge?

> And who would not be offended? I myself have been offended more than once, even unto the deepest abyss of desperation; nay, so far, as even to wish that I had never been born a man; that is, before I was brought to know how healthful that desperation was, and how near it was unto grace.[27]

Nonetheless, that man should be offended does not lead Luther to tamper with the truth of Scripture. God is sovereign and omniscient. Man is not free, although his sins are his own, not God's, for man is not forced to sin.

Having demolished the arguments of Erasmus, Luther contends for the grace of God against free will. He demonstrates the truth from Scripture that all men are depraved, guilty, and incapable of doing or willing good. Man's salvation is all of grace. Man merits nothing. His righteousness is from Christ, imputed freely and by grace.

Hence Luther reveals the seriousness of the matter when he writes, "And I would also, that the advocates for 'Free-will' be admonished in this place, that when they assert 'Free-will,' they are deniers of Christ. For if I obtain grace by my own endeavours, what need have I of the grace of Christ for the receiving of my grace?"[28] And again, "And thus, while you establish 'Free-will,' you make Christ void, and bring the whole Scripture to destruction. And though you may pretend, verbally, that you confess Christ; yet, in reality and in heart, you deny Him."[29]

So far Martin Luther, defender of the irresistible, saving grace of God in Christ.

15

Luther on Justification

Ronald Hanko

Entering Paradise: The Origin of Luther's Doctrine

It is impossible to talk about Luther's doctrine of justification without also talking about Luther's experience of justification. Doctrine and the experience and enjoyment of the blessings of God always go together. This was especially and remarkably true in the case of Luther. His doctrine of justification was the fruit of his coming by grace and by faith to know his own justification before God.

He tells the story of his own spiritual pilgrimage:

> Though I lived as a monk without reproach, I felt that I was a sinner before God with an extremely disturbed conscience. I could not believe that he was placated by my satisfaction. I did not love, yes, I hated the righteous God who punishes sinners, and secretly, if not blasphemously, certainly murmuring greatly, I was angry with God, and said, "As if, indeed, it is not enough, that miserable sinners, eternally lost through original sin, are crushed by every kind of calamity by the law of the decalogue, without having God add pain to pain by the gospel and also by the gospel threatening us with his righteousness and wrath!" Thus I raged with fierce and troubled conscience. Nevertheless, I beat importunately upon Paul at that place, most ardently desiring to know what St. Paul wanted.
>
> At last, by the mercy of God, meditating day and night, I gave heed to the context of the words, namely, "In it the righteousness of God is

revealed, as it is written, 'He who through faith is righteous shall live.'" There I began to understand that the righteousness of God is that by which the righteous lives by a gift of God, namely by faith. And this is the meaning: the righteousness of God is revealed by the gospel, namely, the passive righteousness with which merciful God justifies us by faith, as it is written, "He who through faith is righteous shall live." Here I felt that I was altogether born again and had entered paradise itself through open gates.[1]

This implies that the Reformation did not really begin with the posting of his Ninety-five Theses, but with the reformation of Luther's own life, with a great and gracious work of God in Luther's own soul. It did not begin with a protest against abuses in the church, but with a God-given and biblical answer to Luther's own desperate question, "What must I do to be saved?" So it is always.

No Fishing in Front of the Net: The Crucial Importance of Luther's Doctrine

As a result of his own experience, Luther believed that the doctrine of justification was fundamental. It was for him the doctrine by which the church stands or falls. He considered the teaching of this doctrine of far greater importance than reform of practice and ritual in the church, and he insisted that the reform in other areas would follow if the doctrine were brought home to the hearts of God's people:

> We...beg and urge you most earnestly not to deal first with changes in the ritual, which are dangerous, but to deal with them later. You should deal first with the center of our teaching and fix in the people's minds what they must know about our justification; that is, that it is an extrinsic [external] righteousness—indeed it is Christ's—given to us through faith which comes by grace to those who are first terrified by the law and who, struck by the consciousness of their sins, ardently seek redemption...Adequate reform of ungodly rites will come of itself, however, as soon as the fundamentals of our teaching, having been successfully communicated, have taken root in devout

hearts. These devout people will at once recognize what a great abomination and blasphemy that papistic idol is, namely, the mass and other abuses of the sacrament, so that it will not be necessary to fish in front of the net, that is, first to tear down the ritual before the righteousness of faith is understood.[2]

Reformation often fails because those who seek it do not remember that reformation of doctrine is first and fundamental, especially of such doctrines as these. They cry against abuses but show little or no interest in the doctrines of the church, and are even willing to see those doctrines compromised and cast aside, as the doctrine of justification has been by many evangelicals.[3] Luther was right. Reformation of doctrine will bring reformation of life, but attacking various abuses will not bring reformation at all; it will be as vain as the kind of fishing Luther describes.

The Sweet Exchange: Luther's Understanding of Justification

At the heart of Luther's understanding of justification lies the "sweet exchange." He explains it thus:

> Therefore...learn Christ and him crucified. Learn to praise him and, despairing of yourself, say, "Lord Jesus, you are my righteousness, just as I am your sin. You have taken upon yourself what is mine and have given to me what is yours. You have taken upon yourself what you were not, and have given to me what I was not."[4]

That exchange of our sins for Christ's righteousness, Luther understood to be by imputation. Our sins are *charged* to Christ and his righteousness *charged* to our account. Thus he was *made sin* for us and we were *made righteousness* in him (1 Cor. 5:21), the blessed result being that Christ is treated as Sinner in our place, and we treated as Righteous for his sake. Luther rejected the Romish teaching that righteousness is infused or planted in us and that on account of the resultant change of life we are justified. That, of course, is just another kind of works-righteousness.

According to Luther, righteousness is given as a gift to him who is in fact still a sinner, and the one who receives that gift of righteousness is not yet cured of his sin. He is, when justified, at the same time both sinner and righteous (*simul iustus et peccator*):

> We are in truth and totally sinners, with regard to ourselves and our first birth. Contrariwise, in so far as Christ has been given for us, we are holy and just totally. Hence from different aspects we are said to be just and sinners at one and the same time.[5]

Luther, therefore, often referred to this righteousness by which we are justified as an "alien" righteousness, a righteousness which comes from beyond this world, and which is unattainable by any human effort or merit. It is not only the righteousness of Christ, but also of God in Christ. God gives us his own righteousness and Christ brings it, exchanging it for our sins, a sweet exchange indeed.

The Wedding Ring of Faith: Passive Justification

The exchange of our sins for Christ's perfect righteousness, according to Luther, takes place through faith:

> By the wedding ring of faith [Christ] shares in the sins, death, and pains of hell which are his bride's. As a matter of fact, he makes them his own and acts as if they were his own and as if he himself had sinned; he suffered, died, and descended into hell that he might overcome them all. Now since it was such a one who did all this, and death and hell could not swallow him up, these were necessarily swallowed up by him in a mighty duel; for his righteousness is greater than the sins of all men, his life stronger than death, his salvation more invincible than hell. Thus the believing soul by means of the pledge of its faith is free in Christ, its bridegroom, free from all sins, secure against death and hell, and is endowed with the eternal righteousness, life, and salvation of Christ its bridegroom. So he takes to

himself a glorious bride, "without spot or wrinkle, cleansing her by the washing of water with the word" (cf. Eph. 5:26, 27) of life, that is, by faith in the Word of life, righteousness, and salvation. In this way he marries her in faith, steadfast love, and in mercies, righteousness, and justice, as Hosea 2:19, 20 says.[6]

According to Luther, that faith by which we are justified is entirely a work of God, and in no sense a work of man. By way of emphasizing this, he often described justifying faith as passive:

> For between these two kinds of righteousness, the active righteousness of the Law and the passive righteousness of Christ, there is no middle ground. Therefore he who has strayed away from this Christian righteousness will necessarily relapse into the active righteousness; that is, when he has lost Christ, he must fall into a trust in his own works.[7]

By the use of the word "passive," however, Luther did not mean that justifying faith is without any activity at all. He did not deny that faith is believing and trusting, resting and relying upon Christ. Nevertheless, he believed that faith was first and foremost union with Christ, the marriage of Christ and the believer by which they become one flesh, the union through which the sins of the believer are actually transferred to Christ and the righteousness of Christ given to the believer.[8]

Luther's emphasis continues to serve as a necessary antidote to the current teaching that makes faith another work. He was much nearer the truth than those who deny gracious justification by speaking of faith as a decision of man's own will or by suggesting that faith is man's response to a "well-meant offer" of salvation in the gospel. Of this Luther would have nothing:

> For faith is a divine work which God demands of us; but at the same time He Himself must implant it in us, for we cannot believe by ourselves.[9]

> Faith is not the human notion and dream that some people call

faith... This is due to the fact that when they hear the gospel, they get busy and by their own powers create an idea in their heart which says, "I believe"; they take this then to be a true faith. But, as it is a human figment and idea that never reaches the depths of the heart, nothing comes of it either, and no improvement follows.[10]

Faith is grace, a gift of God, not man's work. What a lost truth today!

All the Rungs of the Ladder: Justification by Faith Alone

By way of defending gracious justification, Luther spoke of justification by faith alone. That one word *alone* (Latin: *sola*) was at the heart of his theology. It is not an exaggeration to say that the Reformation was a battle over that one word, a word that distinguished the Reformation doctrine of justification from that of Rome. The loss of that one word marks the decline of the Reformation these days.

His emphasis on the word *alone* is seen in Luther's German translation of the New Testament. As a result of his own struggles to come to an understanding of Romans 3:28, Luther, in his translation of the book of Romans, added the word *alone* to the passage. In answer to the many criticisms he endured for this translation, he insisted that although the word was not found in the Greek or Latin it nevertheless expressed the meaning of the verse.

> Here in Romans 3:28, I knew very well that the word *solum* is not in the Greek or Latin text; the papists did not have to teach me that. It is a fact that these four letters *sola* are not there. And these blockheads stare at them like cows at a new gate. At the same time they do not see that it conveys the sense of the text; it belongs there if the translation is to be clear and vigorous.[11]

Although the word *alone* was indeed the gate into paradise for Luther, he insisted that it was really not a new gate but a very old one—the gate pointed out by the best of the church fathers and by Paul. He was right. The opposition between grace and works is the opposition between faith and works (Rom. 11:6; Rom. 4:16).

By this word *alone,* however, Luther not only meant to exclude all works from the justification of the sinner, but also meant to emphasize that salvation, of which justification was the heart, was by grace alone and therefore also through Christ alone.

> [Christ] must be all—the beginning, the middle, and the end of our salvation. He must be the first stone, the stone on which other stones are placed and on which the entire vault or roof is constructed. He is the first, the middle, and the last rung of the ladder to heaven (Gen. 28:12). For through Him we must make the beginning, continue, and conclude our journey into yonder life.[12]

His doctrine of justification, therefore, was born not just out of his own experience of that free and gracious gift of God's righteousness, but also out of his love for Christ, the only Savior.

Milking a Billy Goat with a Sieve: The Error of Works-righteousness Rejected

We have examined the essential points of Luther's Reformed and reforming doctrine of justification. Now we will look at some supplementary points, including his opposition to the pernicious doctrine of justification by works. In his own inimitable way he expresses his opposition to the doctrine of justification by works:

> Trying to be justified through the Law, therefore, is as though someone who is already weak and sick were to ask for some even greater trouble that would kill him completely but meanwhile were to say that he intends to cure his disease by this very means; or as though someone suffering from epilepsy were to catch the plague in addition; or as though a leper were to come to another leper, or a beggar to

another beggar, with the aim of giving him assistance and making him rich. As the proverb says, one of these is milking a billy goat and the other is holding the sieve![13]

This means that any talk of works in connection with justification is an attempt to cure man's disease with the disease itself—to cure his wicked working by more works. How angry he would be, therefore, to find that the majority of today's evangelicals are doing just that by making faith itself a work. Luther knew from experience that it could not possibly be so.

Then there is the teaching, so very common today, which makes of faith a decision or act of a man's free will. It suggests that faith, the only requirement for justification, must proceed from man, and it entirely forgets what Ephesians 2:8-10 says about faith. That teaching comes in the guise of "well-meant offers" of salvation, altar calls, decision theology, and such like, and it accompanies the notion that salvation is available to all by Christ's death. It is as much the death of all true theology as was the Romish doctrine of salvation by other works.

Luther points out the error of this kind of thinking:

> The person who believes that he can obtain grace by doing what is in him adds sin to sin, so that he becomes doubly guilty.[14]
>
> But who can bear this blasphemy, that our works beget us or that we are the creatures of our works? In that case it would be permissible to say, contrary to the prophet, "We have made ourselves, and God has not created us" (Mal. 2:10; Ps. 100:3).[15]

Gerhard Forde correctly analyzes this modern form of work righteousness:

> Theology tries to describe accurately what the situation is, but in the fallen world descriptions always turn into prescriptions. Then they become deadly, especially when they turn up in sermons! So, talk of humility, or faith, or grace tends invariably to slip over into prescriptions for what we are to do to make ourselves as humble as possible, or to get some faith, or to decide for grace, and so on. In the theolo-

gy of the cross, however, the point is that the language is to be used in such a way that every prescription is cut off... Thus the impetuous question of whether or not humbling oneself or falling down and praying for grace is "doing something" can only be turned back on the questioner: "When you humble yourself and plead for grace, are you making the claim that you are doing something? If so, you are not pleading for grace, but only your own cause. And so you are still lost. Give up and believe the gospel!"[16]

Like a Beast between Two Riders: The Bondage of the Will

The chief reason Luther rejected the idea that faith is a work of man was his belief in the bondage of the will. Unlike most Christians today, he completely rejected the idea that the will of fallen man could ever act autonomously.

> Man's will is like a beast standing between two riders. If God rides, it wills and goes where God wills... If Satan rides, it wills and goes where Satan wills. Nor may it choose to which rider it will run, or which it will seek; but the riders themselves fight to decide who shall have and hold it.[17]

Faith cannot, therefore, be an act of man's will, a decision for Christ or a choosing between God and Satan, between salvation and damnation, between heaven and hell.

At this point, therefore, Luther differs the most from modern Christianity. The church today, for the most part, has gone back to the doctrine of Rome and Erasmus. The sad thing is, of course, that the modern church has not only gone back to Rome's doctrine of the will, but also, as a result, is on its way back to Rome's doctrine of justification. There are prominent evangelical leaders like James Packer who cannot distinguish between Rome's doctrine and that of historic, biblical Protestantism.

Modern Protestantism's doctrine is not exactly the same as Rome's doctrine of justification by works, but it is much more subtle and dangerous than that of Rome. It is the teaching that salvation is of man's willing, where Rome teaches that it is of man's running, both just different forms of what Luther considered blasphemy against God's mercy (Rom. 9:16).

No Holidays: No Faith without Works

By way of emphasizing that faith is not another work, but a gift of God, Luther often said that we have nothing at all to do in our justification:

> Thesis 25. He is not righteous who does much, but he who, without work, believes much in Christ.
> Thesis 26. The law says, "do this," and it is never done. Grace says, "believe in this," and everything is already done.[18]

In spite of the fact that some of Luther's associates misunderstood him and fell into antinomianism and libertinism, denying good works altogether, Luther himself never had any sympathy for such teaching. Although we, said Luther, have nothing at all to do *for* our justification, there is much that we do as a *result* of justification.

> For it [faith] surely must not be such a sluggish, useless, deaf, or dead thing; it must be a living, productive tree which yields fruit. Therefore this is the test, and this is the difference between faith that is genuine and faith that is false and colored: where faith is true, it manifests itself in life. A false faith, to be sure, bears the same name, employs the same words, and boasts of the same things; but nothing results from it.[19]
>
> Where faith is of the right kind, there deeds also follow; and the greater the faith, the greater the deeds. Faith of the right kind is indeed something powerful, mighty, and active. To it nothing is impossible; nor does it take a rest or take a holiday.[20]

How few there are today who are so taught of God—who can stand firmly against all efforts to make of faith another work, but who can also stand against those who think that any mention of works is a denial of grace.

The Only Organs of the Christian: Faith by Hearing

In his desire to preserve the doctrine of free and gracious justification, justification by faith alone, Luther emphasized very strongly that the chief action of justifying faith is to hear the word. The Christian, for Luther, is most emphatically "all ears":

> But the word "ears" is emphatic and forceful to an extraordinary degree; for in the new law all those countless burdens of the ceremonies, that is, dangers of sins, have been taken away. God no longer requires the feet or the hands or any other member; He requires only the ears. To such an extent has everything been reduced to an easy way of life. For if you ask a Christian what the work is by which he becomes worthy of the name "Christian," he will be able to give absolutely no other answer than that it is the hearing of the Word of God, that is, faith. Therefore the ears alone are the organs of a Christian man, for he is justified and declared to be a Christian, not because of the works of any member but because of faith.[21]

Timothy George suggests that: "*Fides ex auditu,* 'faith out of hearing,' 'faith by means of listening,' is perhaps the best summary of [Luther's] Reformation discovery."[22]

Why did Luther place so much emphasis on hearing the word of God, to the extent at times of identifying faith and hearing? The answer seems plain. On the one hand, Luther wanted to make it as clear as possible that faith is from God and not from man himself. If it comes by hearing, it *must* come from God. On the other hand, over against the idea that faith is some kind of substitute work, Luther emphasized in this way the "passiveness" of justifying faith. It *works* nothing; it only hears. The Christian, the believer, is *all* ears.

Plagued by the Devil: The Necessity of Being Justified

Because he had learned the truth of justification through long spiritual searching and struggling, Luther insisted that only those who are in fact justified by faith and who by faith know Christ and take refuge in him can understand and receive the biblical doctrine of justification. Any other faith than true justifying faith is no faith at all and cannot profit:

> I say that, if we are ever to stand before God with a right and uncolored faith, we must come to the point where we learn clearly to distinguish and separate between ourselves, our life, and Christ the mercy seat. But he who will not do this, but immediately runs headlong to the judgment seat, will find it all right and get a good knock on the head. I have been there myself and was so burnt that I was glad I was able to come to the mercy seat.[23]

Luther has reference here, of course, to faith which thinks itself self-produced, and which believes itself to be "doing something." Such faith cannot find the mercy seat—cannot find Christ—and only gets "knocked on the head."

Not only was Luther's love for the doctrine of justification the result of his own experience (it was for him, as we have seen, the "gate of paradise"), but his opposition to any hint of works-righteousness was also the fruit of his own spiritual struggles. He knew the spiritual danger posed by false doctrine to deceitful human hearts:

> Whoever is interested may learn a lesson from my example, which I shall now confess. A few times—when I did not bear this principal teaching in mind—the devil caught up with me and plagued me with Scripture passages until heaven and earth became too small for me. Then all the works and laws of man were right, and not an error was to be found in the whole papacy. In short, the only one who had ever erred was Luther. All my best works, teaching, sermons, and books had to be condemned. The abominable Mohammed almost became my prophet, and both Turks and Jews were on the way to pure sainthood. Therefore, dear brother, be not proud or smug, and certain that you know Christ well. You hear what I confess to you, admitting

what the devil was able to do against Luther, who is supposed to be a doctor in this art, who has preached, composed, written, said, sung, and read so much in these matters but must still remain a student and sometimes may not be either master or student. So take my advice, and do not celebrate too soon. Are you still standing? Then see that you do not fall (1 Cor. 10:12)![24]

A timely warning indeed!

He pointed out, too, that not only the believer, but also the church must ensure that it does not lose this doctrine:

> If the article on justification hadn't fallen, the brotherhoods, pilgrimages, masses, invocation of saints, etc., would have found no place in the church. If it falls again (which may God prevent!), these idols will return.[25]

Too many churches, once standing, have begun to fall through loss of this doctrine in the teaching of the church and in the consciousness of its members. With Luther we ask, "Are you still standing? Then see that you do not fall."[26]

16

Calvin on Justification

Mark Shand

A man is said to be justified in the sight of God when in the judgment of God he is deemed righteous, and is accepted on account of his righteousness; for as iniquity is abominable to God, so neither can the sinner find grace in his sight, so far as he is and so long as he is regarded as a sinner. Hence, wherever sin is, there also are the wrath and vengeance of God. He, on the other hand, is justified who is regarded not as a sinner, but as righteous, and as such stands acquitted at the judgment-seat of God, where all sinners are condemned...A man will be *justified by faith* when, excluded from the righteousness of works, he by faith lays hold of the righteousness of Christ, and clothed in it appears in the sight of God not as a sinner, but as righteous. Thus we simply interpret justification, as the acceptance with which God receives us into his favor as if we were righteous; and we say that this justification consists in the forgiveness of sins and the imputation of the righteousness of Christ.[1]

JUSTIFICATION BY FAITH ALONE WAS THE FUNDAMENTAL distinguishing doctrine of the sixteenth-century Protestant Reformation. All of the reformers regarded to be of central and paramount importance. Luther declared this doctrine to be the article of the standing or falling church.[2] and contended that nothing "can be given up or compromised [nor can any believer concede or permit anything contrary to it], even if heaven and earth and things temporal should be destroyed."[3]

Calvin on Justification

Calvin described justification as "the main hinge on which religion turns" and also "the principle of the whole doctrine of salvation and of the foundation of all religion."[4] At the outset of his treatment of justification in his *Institutes of the Christian Religion*, Calvin again emphasized the fundamental importance of this doctrine.

> The doctrine of Justification is now to be fully discussed, and discussed under the conviction, that as it is the principal ground on which religion must be supported, so it requires greater care and attention. For unless you understand first of all what your position is before God, and what the judgment which he passes upon you, you have no foundation on which your salvation can be laid, or on which piety towards God can be reared.[5]

There was no significant difference among the reformers in their essential understanding of this doctrine. The unity of thought and expression is reflected in the various formulations of justification in the Reformed creeds.[6]

The reformers developed their understanding of this doctrine in opposition to the doctrine of justification espoused by the Church of Rome. The essence of the charge that the reformers directed at the Church of Rome was that while she proclaimed accurately who Christ was and what he had accomplished with respect to the salvation of sinners, nonetheless, she perverted the gospel of the grace of God by maintaining erroneous and unscriptural views of the grounds on which, and the process through which, the blessings that Christ had procured on the cross were conveyed to sinners. At issue was whether justification was wholly attributable to the grace of God and to the work of Jesus Christ or whether it was proper to ascribe to men and to their powers an active and contributory part in their salvation.

Rome's position with respect to justification had been crafted throughout the Middle Ages, with care being taken to maintain consistency with her underlying semi-Pelagian thinking, which provided for the effective freedom of man's will in salvation. Alhough Rome's views on justification were many years prior to the Reformation, they were not given official sanction until the Council of Trent (1543-1563). The pronouncements of Trent on justification are characterized by vagueness, perhaps designedly so.

Trent's treatment of justification centers in the meaning of the term. Trent defines justification as "a translation, from that state wherein man is born a child of the first Adam, to the state of grace, and of the adoption of the sons of God, through the second Adam, Jesus Christ, our Savior."[7] As the definition suggests, Rome views justification as incorporating the whole process of change that takes place in a man as regards his salvation, including his deliverance from guilt and depravity. That position is made even plainer when Trent defines justification to be "not remission of sins merely, but also the sanctification and renewal of the inward man, through the voluntary reception of the grace, and of the gifts."[8] The result is a confounding of justification and sanctification, with justification comprehending not only the remission of sin and deliverance from the guilt of sin, but also the sanctification or renovation of a man's moral nature.

According to Rome, the ground of justification lies, at least in part, in the inherent righteousness of the sinner and in his good works, the requisite grace being infused into the sinner. Therefore, inherent personal righteousness is the cause of justification, and baptism is the instrument by which it is communicated to the sinner. "If any one saith, that the justice received is not preserved and also increased before God through good works; but that the said works are merely the fruits and signs of Justification obtained, but not a cause of the increase thereof: let him be anathema."[9] For Rome, justification is a cooperative effort involving both God and man.

Accordingly, Rome denies that sinners are justified by faith alone, faith being defined as "the beginning of human salvation, the foundation and the root of all justification."[10] By this Rome means that faith justifies in the sense that it is the chief means for producing that personal righteousness which is the true cause or ground of justification.

> If any one saith, that by faith alone the impious is justified, in such wise as to mean, that nothing else is required to co-operate in order to the obtaining the grace of Justification, and that it is not in any way necessary, that he be prepared and disposed by the movement of his own will: let him be anathema.[11]

Rome's confounding of justification and sanctification also naturally led to the conclusion that justification is not an instantaneous act, but that it involves a gradual process that may not be completed even in this life.

Now that is a soul-destroying doctrine! There was and is no comfort in Rome's view of justification, no assurance of salvation, and no confirmation that a sinner is right with God. It is no wonder that Luther despaired when, in keeping with Rome's dogma, he mistakenly concluded that "the righteousness of God," in Romans 1:17, referred to God's righteous anger against sin. Luther was able to find solace only when he came to understand that "the righteousness of God" in Romans 1:17 did not refer to the attribute of God's righteousness, but rather to the righteousness that God graciously and freely gives to the sinner on account of Jesus Christ.

Like Luther, Calvin recognized the comfortless nature of Rome's doctrine of justification. Speaking of Rome's confusion of justification with sanctification and its consequential destruction of a believer's comfort, Calvin writes:

> But as it is too well known by experience, that the remains of sin always exist in the righteous, it is necessary that justification should be something very different from reformation to newness of life. This latter God begins in his elect, and carries on during the whole course of life, gradually and sometimes slowly, so that if placed at his judgment-seat they would always deserve sentence of death. He justifies not partially, but freely, so that they can appear in the heavens as if clothed with the purity of Christ. No portion of righteousness could pacify the conscience. It must be decided that we are pleasing to God, as being without exception righteous in his sight. Hence it follows that the doctrine of justification is perverted and completely overthrown whenever doubt is instilled into the mind, confidence in sal-

vation is shaken, and free and intrepid prayer is retarded; yea, whenever rest and tranquillity with spiritual joy are not established.[12]

The vagueness that characterizes Trent's position on justification and the comfortless nature of its pronouncements stand in sharp contrast to the clarity, simplicity, and warmth of the writings of Calvin and the other reformers on this subject. Calvin's view of justification can be summarized in the following three propositions:

First, justification is an act of God's free grace, and as a forensic or legal act it does not change the inner nature of a man, but only the judicial relationship in which he stands before God—God's accepting him as righteous in his sight.

Second, the ground for justification is not found in the inherent righteousness of the believer, but only in the imputed righteousness of Jesus Christ, which a sinner appropriates by faith—faith being that God-given power whereby the believer is united to Jesus Christ and becomes partaker of all his benefits, including having his righteousness put to his account.

Third, justification is not a progressive work of God; rather it is a single, instantaneous act of God whereby the sinner is declared to be without guilt, so that the believer can be absolutely certain that his state before God is no longer one of wrath and condemnation, but one of favor and acceptance.

Calvin identified justification as a legal or forensic concept, distinct from sanctification. As such, Calvin viewed justification as the changing of a man's legal state before God, but not his inner nature. Justification resulted in the declaration by God that a sinner was without guilt, in light of his having been clothed in the righteousness of Jesus Christ.

> Let us now consider the truth of what was said in the definition—viz. that justification by faith is reconciliation with God, and that this consists solely in the remission of sins. We must always return to the axiom, that the wrath of God lies upon all men so long as they continue sinners. This is elegantly expressed by Isaiah in these words: "Behold, the Lord's hand is not shortened, that it cannot save; nei-

ther his ear heavy, that it cannot hear: but your iniquities have separated between you and your God, and your sins have hid his face from you, that he will not hear" (Isa. 59:1, 2). We are here told that sin is a separation between God and man; that His countenance is turned away from the sinner; and that it cannot be otherwise, since to have any intercourse with sin is repugnant to his righteousness...When the Lord, therefore, admits him to union, he is said to justify him, because he can neither receive him into favor, nor unite him to himself, without changing his condition [legal standing] from that of a sinner into that of a righteous man. We add that this is done by remission of sins. For if those whom the Lord has reconciled to himself are estimated by works, they will still prove to be in reality sinners, while they ought to be pure and free from sin. It is evident, therefore, that the only way in which those whom God embraces are made righteous, is by having their pollutions wiped away by the remission of sins, so that this justification may be termed in one word the remission of sins.[13]

Calvin maintained a clear and sharp distinction between justification and sanctification. However, he acknowledged that a radical change of character invariably accompanied justification.

> We dream not of a faith which is devoid of good works, nor of a justification which can exist without them: the only difference is, that while we acknowledge that faith and works are necessarily connected, we, however, place justification in faith, not in works. How this is done is easily explained, if we turn to Christ only, to whom our faith is directed and from whom it derives all its power. Why, then, are we justified by faith? Because by faith we apprehend the righteousness of Christ, which alone reconciles us to God. This faith, however, you cannot apprehend without at the same time apprehending sanctification...Christ, therefore, justifies no man without also sanctifying him. These blessings are conjoined by a perpetual and inseparable tie.[14]

Calvin asserted that justification was by faith alone. By faith alone, Calvin did not mean that faith itself justified, but rather that faith was the instrument by which the believer was united to Christ and by which he appropriated Jesus Christ and his righteousness.

The Reformed doctrine of justification by faith alone is essential to salvation. Therefore, it is disturbing to note that presently in North America and in Great Britain, among those who profess to hold to the Reformed faith, there is renewed debate regarding the teaching of Scripture on this subject. What warrants very close scrutiny are the ominously familiar attempts to develop a view of justification that is no longer by faith alone, but by faith and works. Reformed churches ought to bear in mind the note of warning issued by Francis Turretin with respect to the adulteration of justification by faith alone, a doctrine that he styled as of the principal rampart of the Christian religion. "This being adulterated or subverted, it is impossible to retain purity of doctrine in other places."[15]

17

Rome's Dreadful Doctrine of Purgatory

Kenneth Koole

OTHER THAN THE WORSHIP OF THE VIRGIN MARY, THE doctrine we most associate with the Roman Catholic Church and her abuses is probably her doctrine of purgatory.

This teaching underscores what Rome is all about, namely, ignoring (or better, inventing) Scripture, promoting superstition, inculcating fear into the minds of her members, using fear to extract a steady stream of income, corrupting the gospel of Christ crucified, and destroying the blessed assurance of faith in him.

This doctrine makes plain from just what a bondage God used the Reformation to deliver his people once more.

The striking thing about this purgatory is that it is not the place of the damned, but, according to Rome, the place of the redeemed. It is where all children of God go (except for an elite, super-pious few), there to suffer agonies and torments not at all unlike those of hell itself. The only difference between the two has to do with duration, hell's torments being eternal, but purgatory's eventually coming to an end. Still, for many these sufferings are said to last for centuries. Relief from the agony of the fires of purgatory is not meant to come easily for those who die good members of Rome.

The Manual of the Purgatorial Society states:

> According to the Holy Fathers of the Church, the fire of purgatory does not differ from the fire of hell, except in point of duration. "It is the same fire," says St. Thomas Aquinas, "that torments the reprobate in hell, and the just in purgatory. The least pain in purgatory," he says, "surpasses the greatest suffering in this life." Nothing but the eternal duration makes the fire of hell more terrible than that of purgatory.[1]

In light of the above, one can well understand the great gloom and oppressive grief that marks death and funerals in Romish circles. Death of believers is not to be considered a release from tears and pain, a victory of faith, and an entry into the glory and the bosom of the Lord, but a descent into an abyss, into the crackling of fire, the smell of smoke, and the groans and cries of thirsty, tormented souls. Understandably, at Romish funerals not songs of triumph and joy are heard, but rather somber, doleful laments. Black with veils is the only appropriate dress.

What moved ambitious churchmen to invent the monstrosity of purgatory is not so difficult to ascertain. It looms as a threat, a sizable club to be used against those who have thoughts of resisting the authority of Rome's clergy, and it has proved an endless source of income in return for the promise of an early release.

Rome, of course, has not admitted to this reality and charge. She insists that the doctrine of purgatory is a most beneficial and sanctifying doctrine. The Council of Trent, the official response of Rome to the Reformation, commanded her bishops diligently to see to it that "the sound doctrine concerning purgatory...be believed, maintained, taught, and every where proclaimed by the faithful of Christ."[2]

Rome argues that purgatory is a place of restitution for one's sins. Various kinds of sins make one liable to two sorts of divine punishment, eternal and temporal. Receiving the various sacraments takes care of the eternal punishment, while acts of penance and of good works are meant to deal with temporal punishment. But good works and penance commonly prove a sporadic thing. So purgatory is the place where one makes the final restitution for those evils one's own sporadic good works failed to overcome. There the completion of one's just punishment takes place. Those members of the church who have been lax and careless in living a life devoted to God and the church, and especially in listening to the exhortations of the priest, can expect that restitution to be long and severe indeed. What could be more just than that?

Besides, Rome argues, such a threat will have a sanctifying effect on believers in this life. Knowing what awaits one if one is lax and careless in one's spiritual devotion should put enough fear of the Lord into one to give him strong incentive to refrain from many a temptation and evil. Without this threat, members would simply take advantage of the protecting grace of the church and be inclined to lifelong carelessness.

History has proved how deceptive and spiritually bankrupt Rome's justification of the doctrine has been. The worldliness and immorality of Rome's members, to say nothing of the scandalous behavior of her clergy in every age, has demonstrated again and again how little effect the looming threat of this fictitious purgatory has had on the improvement of the morals, to say nothing of the spirituality, of her members' lives. Threats and dread may produce a bit of restraint in some areas of immorality, but never will such produce spirituality and true godliness. That is the product of heartfelt gratitude. And precious little is thankworthy about the abyss of purgatory.

The wholesale monetary abuse of purgatory by Rome's clergy is too well documented to be refuted. The sale of indulgences is written large on the pages of her sacrilegious history. If one cannot work his way out of purgatory, his relatives can buy his way out of the abyss by contributing sums of money to the church in the name of the dearly departed (or by paying for a solemn mass for the dead). The church claims the authority to determine by how much each contribution shortens one's stay. Of course, how the church is able

The Sixteenth-Century Reformation of the Church

to calculate just how long one was sentenced to suffer in the first place is a great mystery, but when you are dealing with people steeped for centuries in such superstitions, such questions are seldom asked.

The doctrine of purgatory was declared an article of faith by the Council of Florence in 1439, which explains the flurry of indulgences at the time of the Reformation, but it had already received ecclesiastical recognition at the time of Pope Gregory the Great (A.D. 590-604). Although the Reformation soundly denounced the practice, the sore abuse, sad to say, did not end with the Reformation. The ongoing abuse is well chronicled in the autobiography of the Canadian priest, Father Chiniquy, who converted to Protestantism in the 1800s.

> How long, O Lord, shall that insolent enemy of the gospel, the Church of Rome, be permitted to fatten herself upon the tears of the widow and of the orphan by means of that cruel and impious invention of paganism — purgatory?[3]

The "fattening" to which Chiniquy referred was the extorting of money from the vulnerable, the lonely, and those in grief. The church, like the Pharisees of Christ's day, was not above devouring widows' houses.

It scarcely needs mentioning that such a system does not curtail immorality and ungodliness, especially among the wealthy, but promotes it. What need is there of godliness and repentance, when money turns the same trick? The wealthy have an advantage over the poor.

The whole business is a travesty.

Purgatory is an invention without a shred of biblical support. Rome's primary "biblical" support is in one of the apocryphal books, of all things, 2 Maccabees 12. But even this is a doubtful reference. Another so-called proof is 1 Corinthians 3:12-15, which speaks of one's works being tested by fire. But this is a testing of one's works, not a burning of one's soul, and it refers to what will take place on the judgment day, not in some intermediate state. Every other passage Rome uses is as forced and misused as the one in 1 Corinthians.

Further, Rome's doctrine would deprive believers of the blessed word of God that gives them sweet assurance of glory directly upon the experience of death, passages such as John 5:24: "He that heareth my word, and believeth on him that sent me, hath everlasting life, and shall not come into condemnation; but is passed from death unto life." Notice, "…shall not come into condemnation." As Paul declares, for the believer to be "absent from the body" is to be "present with the Lord" (2 Cor. 5:8).

Centrally, as with all of Rome's major doctrinal errors, her teaching of purgatory is a direct assault upon the gospel of Christ crucified, and the power, value, and full sufficiency of his atoning sacrifice for sin. The "once-for-all" character of Christ's death and suffering is mutilated and slandered (see Heb. 9:12, 26-28 and Heb. 10:14, 18). As the apostle John declares, "The blood of Jesus Christ his Son cleanseth us from all sin" (1 John 1:7). Christ Jesus died exactly so that we would not be as those characterized by a "certain fearful looking for of judgment and fiery indignation" (Heb. 10:27).

In the name of the gospel and the full sufficiency of Christ's atonement for everyone who believes, the dreadful fiction of purgatory must be denounced and dismissed. Rome ought to pay special heed to the scathing words of the apostle Peter—said to be her first pope—to Simon the magician who also thought spiritual things could be purchased with money: "Thy money perish with thee" (Acts 8:20).

18

Piety and the Reformation, or the Reformation's Awed Love of God

David J. Engelsma

IF WE WERE TO UNDERSTAND CHRISTIAN PIETY MERELY AS decent behavior, we would have to say that the sixteenth-century Reformation of the church did not have piety as its purpose. This is startling because the conduct of the members of the Roman Catholic Church was scandalous. Both laity and clergy were worldly and immoral. The holiness the church boasted of was foolish and worthless: pilgrimages, crusades, worship of relics, celibacy (rejection of marriage in favor of fornication and concubinage), and indulgences.

The Reformation was not a reformation of morals. The reformers themselves made this clear. In his early work, *The Freedom of a Christian*, Martin Luther wrote:

> I have, to be sure, sharply attacked ungodly doctrines in general, and I have snapped at my opponents, not because of their bad morals, but because of their ungodliness...I have no quarrel with any man concerning his morals but only concerning the word of truth.[1]

John Calvin agreed. Writing to the Roman Catholic cardinal Sadoleto, Calvin stated:

> It is scarcely possible that the minds of the common people should not be greatly alienated from you by the many examples of cruelty,

avarice, intemperance, arrogance, insolence, lust, and all sorts of wickedness, which are openly manifested by men of your order, but none of those things would have driven us to the attempt which we made under a much stronger necessity. That necessity was, that the light of divine truth had been extinguished, the word of God buried, the virtue of Christ left in profound oblivion, and the pastoral office subverted.[2]

Rome understands well that the purpose of the Reformation was not improvement of morals. In his history of the Reformation, Roman Catholic historian Henri Daniel-Rops correctly declares concerning Luther:

> Nor did he make his protest in order to reform ecclesiastical morals. Luther himself roundly asserted that such had never been his aim...The problem of reform, in the sense understood by so many men of the age, was of secondary importance to Luther...The revolution he desired to effect was neither social, nor political, nor ecclesiastical, but theological.[3]

This is not to say that the reformers had no concern for the lives of Christians and for the reformation of life. Certainly they did. But their concern was deeper. It went to the root of the immorality. The Reformation was radical. Its radical purpose was a restoration of the right worship and service of God by man and thus the glory of God in his church. The right worship and service of God is the activity of the man who knows and reverences God. This reverential knowledge of God is Christian piety. It issues in a holy life. And this was the purpose of the Reformation.

Although the word *piety* occurs only once in the King James Bible—in 1 Timothy 4:7—it would be a mistake to conclude that the Bible does not teach piety, that Reformed Christians need not be pious, or that piety is a characteristic of odd cults, fundamentalists, and little old ladies of both sexes. The Bible teaches piety in other words. The fear of Jehovah in the Old Testament is piety. The Israelite's fear of Jehovah was his reverence for and love of God as the one who redeemed him from Egypt. This fear of Jehovah motivated the Israelite to keep Jehovah's commandments. Everyone who has read the book of Proverbs knows how practical the fear of Jehovah was, and is.

In the New Testament, piety is called "godliness." In 1 Timothy 5:4 every Christian is called to "exercise thyself unto godliness." Verse 8 makes the astounding claim for godliness, or piety, that it is "profitable unto all things, having promise of the life that now is, and of that which is to come." This is powerful incentive for vigorous exercise of oneself unto godliness. In 1 Timothy 3:16, the apostle refers to the central confession of the Christian faith, and the very foundation of the church, as the "mystery of godliness." The coming of the eternal Son of God into human flesh had to do with godliness, or piety. It had piety as its goal.

Biblically, piety is loving reverence for, or, as I should prefer to say, "awed love of," the triune God, the Father of Jesus Christ. Piety is such an adoration of this God as grips and possesses a man. Piety is not one part of the Christian's life, which he puts on, and then puts off, with his Sunday suit. Piety is not even the most important part of his life. Piety *is* his life. The pious man is simply the man who lives *coram Deo*, "in the presence of God."

Piety is a matter of the heart. Therefore, it is willing, free, unconstrained, unforced. The pious man delights in God. Ask him why, and he will answer, "Because God is delightful." The pious man enjoys God, because God is enjoyable.

Piety necessarily works itself out and manifests itself in all of everyday life in the world—in every aspect of the earthly life of the pious, in every human activity and relationship, and in every sphere. Piety cannot be "awed love" of God without any change in one's life. Piety is always active.

To be pious is Reformed, unless the Reformed faith and life are not biblical Christianity. It is an error to suppose that piety is un-Reformed, as though piety were the possession of fundamentalists and mystics. It is a bad sign that we are embarrassed to appear, or be thought, pious. It is ominous that we use the word *pious* only in a bad sense, to describe one who hypocritically affects piety by trivial, external acts and by an outward appearance of black suit and somber countenance. We should call such appearance and such actions "pietistic."

It is the need of the hour for Reformed churches and Reformed church members that we exercise ourselves unto piety. Impiety abounds, the same impiety that disfigured the pre-Reformation church: corruption of the public worship of God with regard to preaching, administration of the sacraments, discipline, and liturgy; formalism in worship; refusal to worship, as is evident in the poor attendance at the services of worship; disinterest in the things of God, as manifested by the forgetting of the Sabbath day, to profane it; worldliness; the love of money, the love of pleasures rather than the love of God; wicked unfaithfulness to God's marriage ordinance by divorce and remarriage; drunkenness and debauched partying; the amusing of themselves by professing Reformed Christians with vile songs, corrupt movies, depraved books, and rotten television programs; and living, year after year, in hatred of and enmity with a neighbor.

Even for the congregation, believer, and child of believers who are living piously, being pious is a constant battle.

It is important, therefore, to know that piety comes from the Spirit of Christ. We cannot produce it in ourselves. To think so is disbelief of the Reformation's message that salvation is by grace alone. As we use the Spirit's means—preaching and sacraments—we must beseech God for the presence and power of the Spirit with and by these means.

Although piety is a gift of the Spirit, true piety is not a "piety of the Spirit," that is, mystical experiences, ecstatic feelings, and strange behavior supposedly due to the direct influence of the Spirit. The Reformation condemned this false spirituality as another form of un-Christian impiety (read Luther's diatribe "Against the Heavenly Prophets").[4]

Genuine piety is a "piety of the Word." If a man is to love and reverence God, he must know God as the great, good, glorious God of his salvation in Jesus Christ. God gives this knowledge of himself only in the doctrine of Scripture. This doctrine is the gospel of grace, at the heart of which is the promise of the forgiveness of sins, in the mercy of God, on the basis only of the cross, for every sinner who believes for righteousness, and believes only.

By the preaching of this gospel, the Spirit works piety. The preaching of sound doctrine—this is what we need, if we are to be pious. This is not the same as dry, abstract, theoretical discourses on doctrine. There is a preaching of doctrine that, although orthodox, or at least not heterodox, is of no real use to God's people: arid discussion of dogma; bitter, endlessly sustained polemics against errors that are no danger to the congregation; and brilliant speculation about points of theology far removed from the people. Such preaching is invariably the occasion for pietism.

The Reformation wanted nothing of this kind of theology and preaching. Luther wrote: "True theology is practical, and its foundation is Christ, whose death is appropriated to us through faith...Accordingly speculative theology belongs to the devil in hell" (which theology Luther promptly applied to Zwingli).[5]

Calvin was one with Luther in insisting on edifying preaching. In his commentary on 1 Timothy 6:3, particularly the phrase "the doctrine which is according to godliness," Calvin blisters all preaching that is "hypocritical and altogether framed for the purposes of ostentation and of idle display." He adds:

> "Doctrine" will not be consistent with "godliness," if it do not instruct us in the fear and worship of God, if it do not edify our faith, if it do not train us to patience, humility, and all the duties of that love which we owe to our fellowmen. Whoever, therefore, does not strive to teach *usefully*, does not teach as he ought to do; and not only so, but that doctrine is neither godly nor sound, whatever may be the brilliancy of its display, that does not tend to the profit of the hearers.[6]

What the church needs is lively, profitable, practical doctrine—doctrine that aims at the godliness of the congregation.

Piety and the Reformation

The Spirit gives piety by means of doctrine in the way of the congregation's embracing this doctrine by faith.

Piety is born and nourished by faith.

Piety is the gift of the Holy Spirit. The Spirit in a man or a woman is a pious Spirit. We receive the Spirit by faith, as the apostle teaches by his question in Galatians 3:2: "Received ye the Spirit by the works of the law, or by the hearing of faith?"

Piety is the awed love of God that arises from the knowledge of God in his word. It is faith that knows the word, and the God revealed in the word.

Out of the faith that knows and trusts God as one's own gracious heavenly Father in Jesus Christ, one is pious. Just as one is righteous by faith only, so one is pious by faith only. No one is pious by works, by the law, or by dreadful threats and slavish fear.

In his *The Freedom of a Christian*, Luther asked, "What man is there whose heart, upon hearing these things, will not rejoice to its depths, and when receiving such comfort will not grow tender so that he will love Christ as he never could by means of any laws or works?"[7]

Let us apply this to ourselves. Am I disturbed by my own impiety, my formal Christianity, my worldliness, and my lack of spirituality? Do I desire piety? I must hear and believe the word of the cross. I must pray that the Spirit will increase faith in me, apply the gospel to my heart and life, and thus dwell in me more intimately.

As ministers and elders, are we desirous that our congregations be pious? Let us preach Christ crucified, the gospel of sovereign grace, in season and out of season. We are not to preach the law, good works, social reform, or the latest liberal or evangelical fad, but Christ crucified. We are not to proclaim a godliness attained by the people's strenuous efforts as they read, and exert themselves to carry out, as many "how to" religious manuals as possible. Nor are we to teach a godliness achieved by the people's preparing themselves scrupulously for a wonderful second blessing of the Spirit. But we are to preach and teach the godliness that is received by believing, and by believing only.

We must be bold and searching in our preaching. We must bring the gospel home to believers, especially fearful, faint believers, with careful, personal application. In the interests of doing this, we must dare to attack impiety, not only out there in the world and in other churches (which is quite safe), but also in our own congregation (which can become quite dangerous). Preaching grace does not imply that there is never any admonition, never a "sharp sermon." Luther, who abhorred legalism, preached "sharp sermons," as his 1539 sermon "Soberness and Moderation" illustrates.[8]

Aiming at godliness, the word that we bring is the sworn foe of all ungodliness. It destroys impiety, in order to create piety.

For this kind of preaching, we ourselves must be pious men, not only of unblamable conduct outwardly, but also living and working in the presence of God, with awed love of him.

"Take heed," the apostle commands, "unto thyself" (1 Tim. 4:16).

19

Calvin's Doctrine of the Christian Life

David J. Engelsma

JOHN CALVIN'S DESCRIPTION OF THE CHRISTIAN LIFE IN book three of his *Institutes of the Christian Religion* makes every charge that the Reformed faith minimizes holiness of life not so much false as absurd.

What a grand, gripping, humbling, sobering, and moving description of the Christian life this is. It is no wonder that this section of the *Institutes* was very soon published separately and that it still is published in English as a separate booklet, *The Golden Booklet of the Christian Life*.[1]

Ministers must preach this biblical description of the Christian life to the congregations. Preaching the Christian life as Calvin presents it is the preaching of doctrine. It is the preaching of doctrine's necessary and glorious fruits and ends. Calvin expresses the right relation of doctrine and life:

> To doctrine in which our religion is contained we have given the first place, since by it our salvation commences; but it must be transfused into the breast, and pass into the conduct, and so transform us into itself, as not to prove unfruitful.[2]

When ministers preach the Christian life, they should warn the people—and themselves—that "doctrine is not an affair of the tongue, but of the life."[3]

Such is the compressed wisdom, beauty, and power of

Calvin's treatment of the Christian life in this section of the *Institutes* that it defies any adequate summary. One can do justice to it only by reading it in its entirety. I urge every reader to do this: read chapters six through ten of book three of the *Institutes*. In this essay, I call attention briefly to the main lines of this classic pattern of the Christian life according to a Reformed understanding of it, quoting a few of the more striking statements about the Christian life by the reformer.

What Calvin gives is the pattern of the Christian life. He is concerned to "point out the method by which a pious man may be taught how to frame his life aright, and briefly lay down some universal rule by which he may not improperly regulate his conduct."[4] This pattern is drawn from Holy Scripture. The pattern describes how the Spirit works in everyone who is united to Christ by the bond of faith. The Spirit works in such a way that they are called to be active in approximating this pattern.

Because we are active in ordering our life according to the pattern revealed in Scripture and realized by the Spirit, Calvin begins with the motivations for living the Christian life. We should strive to be holy as the God to whom we are united is holy. Our life should express Christ. And every benefit God gives us calls us to an appropriate thankfulness.[5]

With regard to the pattern of the Christian life, Calvin says that, "although the Law of God contains a perfect rule of conduct admirably arranged, it has seemed proper to our divine Master to train his people by a more accurate method, to the rule which is enjoined in the Law." Plainly, the subject is the objective standard, or rule, that forms the Christian life of us all. Calvin holds up the law—the Ten Commandments—as "a perfect rule of conduct admirably arranged." Here is the well-known "third use of the law"— the use of the law as rule of a holy life—characteristic of Calvinism. But the phrase advocating the law as the standard of the Christian life is concessive: "although." The force of the sentence is to promote another, "more accurate method" that will shape us to the Christian life God intends for us. This "more accurate method" is the doctrine found especially in the New Testament, particularly Romans 12, that the elect believer is not his own, but God's. That we belong to God is the implication of the exhortation in Romans 12:1, "Present your bodies a living sacrifice, holy, acceptable unto God."

Even more than the law, the truth of our belonging to God must pattern our life.

> The great point, then, is, that we are consecrated and dedicated to God, and therefore should not henceforth think, speak, design, or act, without a view to his glory...But if we are not our own, but the Lord's, it is plain both what error is to be shunned, and to what end the actions of our lives ought to be directed. We are not our own; therefore, neither is our own reason or will to rule our acts and counsels. We are not our own; therefore, let us not make it our end to seek what may be agreeable to our carnal nature. We are not our own; therefore, as far as possible, let us forget ourselves and the things that are ours. On the other hand, we are God's; let us, therefore, live and die to him.[7]

All that follows in Calvin's description of the Christian life is a thorough, consistent working out of the truth of our belonging to God. In describing the Christian life, Calvin does not explicitly use the law as the rule, but New Testament teachings concerning self-denial, bearing the cross, and the like.

What immediately strikes everyone familiar with the Heidelberg Catechism is that Calvin's rule for the Christian life is the same as the believer's only comfort. The same truth that is the comfort of the gospel—belonging to God—decisively forms and shapes our Christian life.

What will the life be that conforms to the law and more especially to the truth that by the redemption of the cross and the renewal of the Spirit we are not our own but the Lord's?

First, it will be a life of the service of God. "Let this, then, be the first step, to abandon ourselves, and devote the whole energy of our minds to the service of God. By service, I mean not only that which consists in verbal obedience, but that by which the mind, divested of its own carnal feelings, implicitly obeys the call of the Spirit of God."[8]

Second, the Christian life is self-denial. Calvin distinguishes self-denial toward the neighbor and self-denial toward God. With regard to self-denial toward the neighbor, Calvin exposes our wickedness in seeking self and despising the neighbor.[9] He grounds our love of the neighbor in "the image of God, which exists in all, and to which we owe all honour and love."[10] Calvin warns that outward deeds of goodness to the neighbor are not enough. We must have inward, sympathetic love of the needy neighbor. Christians should "put themselves in the place of him whom they see in need of their assistance, and pity his misfortune as if they felt and bore it, so that a feeling of pity and humanity should incline them to assist him just as they would themselves."[11]

Self-denial toward God is resignation of "ourselves and all we have" to the Lord's will.[12] We are to depend only upon God's blessing for the success of our earthly life. We must bear adversity patiently. Describing the troubles of life in vivid detail, Calvin writes that the believer can bear them without cursing God or resisting, because he has "resigned himself entirely to the Lord, placing all the course of his life entirely at his [God's] disposal."[13]

At this point, certain observations are in order. What is this aspect of the Christian life but living our belief and confession of divine sovereignty? How radically different is the Christian's self-denial toward God from the thinking of the world of the ungodly: "Assert yourself!" "Stand up for your rights!"

A third characteristic of the Christian life that the Spirit works in us and that we must strive for according to the pattern of belonging to God is bearing the cross. Calvin tells us that this is an aspect of self-denial. Here I must make a confession. By this point in his description of the Christian life, Calvin has stretched me to my limit, and beyond. I am ready for his "Amen" to the Christian life. Whereupon Calvin says, "The pious mind must ascend still higher."[14]

"Still higher"?

"Still higher"!

"Still higher," because although Calvin has already foretold for us a life of trouble, now he tells us that we must expect to share the sufferings of Christ. This is cross-bearing: sharing the sufferings of Christ. Every one of us, none excepted, must prepare for "a hard, laborious, troubled life, a life full of many and various kinds of evils." The pain of these evils is "the bitterness of the cross," that is, the bitterness of the cross of Christ in our lives.[15]

Our cross is not atoning suffering. Rather, it is our sharing in the hatred and reproach of Christ by the wicked. "In maintaining the truth of God against the lies of Satan, or defending the good and innocent against the injuries of the bad, we are obliged to incur the offence and hatred of the world, so as to endanger life, fortune, or honor."[16] God imposes this cross upon us to prove our sonship: we obey God in love when obedience is painful and costly.

Precious benefits come to us from bearing the cross. The cross teaches us not to depend on our flesh. Through the cross we experience God's faithful help, as we rest on him alone. In response to the cross, we manifest our endurance by grace. The biblical name for this endurance is patience. The cross in our life guards us against wanton rebellion against God, which is the danger when all goes well for the Christian. Calvin sees earthly prosperity as a threat to the Christian life.

> Thus, lest we become emboldened by an over-abundance of wealth; lest elated with honor, we grow proud; lest inflated with other advantages of body, or mind, or fortune, we grow insolent, the Lord himself interferes as he sees to be expedient by means of the cross, subduing and curbing the arrogance of our flesh, and that in various ways as the advantage of each requires.[17]

The cross chastises us for our faults. And the cross bestows honor upon us. To suffer for the sake of Christ and righteousness is "the special badge of his [God's] soldiers."[18] "We now see," says Calvin, "how many advantages are at once produced by the cross."[19]

Although Calvin grants that the cross inflicts real and deep sorrow, which sorrow on our part is not sinful, nevertheless, in view of the benefits of the cross, we can and should bear the cross cheerfully.[20] Indeed, so Calvin concludes, the benefits of the cross enable and require us to be thankful for the cross, with all its bitterness. This is the explanation of the Bible's exhortations to Christians to be thankful for all things, evil things as well as good things. The explanation is not that we enjoy the bitterness. We do not. Nor should we. But we are thankful for the cross in our life in view of the benefits God brings us through the cross.

A fourth characteristic of the life of every Christian, according to Calvin, is contempt for this present earthly life and hopeful meditation upon the future heavenly life—the life that the Christian will enjoy after death and especially upon the return of Christ. This characteristic is related to the preceding inasmuch as tribulation—the cross in one's life—has the unavoidable and salutary effect on the Christian that he learns to despise this life and hope with ardent longing for the coming life.

In urging this characteristic as part of the pattern of the Christian life, Calvin uses vigorous language. He uses language that is much too strong for our age, but language that our age, particularly Reformed saints in our age, very much needs to hear. If we were to address Reformed and Presbyterian people with Calvin's statements on the necessity of holding this earthly life in contempt, without informing them that the statements were those of Calvin, most would respond by screaming, "World-flight!" or "Anabaptist!" They would charge, with the sublimest, unwitting irony, that we lack a "Calvinistic" world-view.

Listen.

> [We must] despise the present, and...aspire to the future life...This life, estimated in itself, is restless, troubled, in numberless ways wretched, and plainly in no respect happy...All we have to seek or hope for here is contest...When we think of the crown we must raise our eyes to heaven...Our mind never rises seriously to desire and

aspire after the future, until it has learned to despise the present life.[21]

> There is no medium between the two things: the earth must either be worthless in our estimation, or keep us enslaved by an intemperate love of it...We [must] hasten to despise the world, and aspire with our whole heart to the future life.[22]

Calvin exercises some sharp spiritual/psychological examination of every one of us.

> Every one of us, indeed, would be thought to aspire and aim at heavenly immortality during the whole course of his life. For we would be ashamed in no respect to excel the lower animals; whose condition would not be at all inferior to ours, had we not a hope of immortality beyond the grave. But when you attend to the plans, wishes, and actions of each, you see nothing in them but the earth. Hence our stupidity; our minds being so dazzled with the glare of wealth, power, and honours, that they can see no farther. The heart also, engrossed with avarice, ambition, and lust, is weighed down and cannot rise above them. In short, the whole soul, ensnared by the allurements of the flesh, seeks its happiness on the earth.[23]

Calvin goes on to explain that we should view this life as preparation for the glory of the heavenly kingdom and, therefore, not make this life the end or goal. He guards against misunderstanding of his exhortation that we despise this life by warning that "contempt" is not hatred of earthly life or ingratitude to God for it. "This life, though abounding in all kinds of wretchedness, is justly classed among divine blessings which are not to be despised." [24]

Viewing earthly life as preparation for the better, heavenly life, the Christian does not tremble in terror of approaching death. Rather, he desires death. "No man has made much progress in the school of Christ who does not look forward with joy to the day of death and final resurrection (2 Tim. 4:18; Titus 2:13)."[25]

In his explanation of the Christian life as cross-bearing and, therefore, a despising of earthly life in hope of the heavenly, Calvin makes plain that he saw no "golden age" of carnal, millennial ease and glory in store for the church in history.

> Thus, indeed, it is; the whole body of the faithful, so long as they live on the earth, must be like sheep for the slaughter, in order that they may be conformed to Christ their head (Rom. 8:36). Most deplorable, therefore, would their situation be did they not, by raising their mind to heaven, become superior to all that is in the world, and rise above the present aspect of affairs (1 Cor. 15:19).[26]

As he suggested when he explained that contempt for earthly life is not ingratitude to God for it, Calvin saw in the New Testament as a fifth characteristic of the Christian life that the Christian uses the benefits of earthly life rightly. In general, this will consist of using "its [the earth's] blessings only in so far as they assist our progress [to the heavenly kingdom], rather than retard it."[27] Following the pattern of the New Testament, Calvin warns against two dangers. One is the binding of the conscience, whether by oneself or by others, with the unbiblical restriction that the Christian may use earthly things only if they are absolutely necessary. In his treatment of Christian liberty, later in the *Institutes*, Calvin expresses the spiritual danger of this ascetic view of the Christian life in a classic statement.

> Many think us absurd in raising a question as to the free eating of flesh, the free use of dress and holidays, and similar frivolous trifles, as they think them; but they are of more importance than is commonly supposed. For when once the conscience is entangled in the net, it enters a long and inextricable labyrinth, from which it is afterwards most difficult to escape. When a man begins to doubt whether it is lawful for him to use linen for sheets, shirts, napkins, and handkerchiefs, he will not long be secure as to hemp, and will at last have doubts as to tow; for he will revolve in his mind whether he cannot sup without napkins, or dispense with handkerchiefs. Should he deem a daintier food unlawful, he will afterwards feel uneasy for using loaf-bread and common eatables, because he will think that his body might possibly be supported on a still meaner food. If he hesitates as to a more genial wine, he will scarcely drink the worst with a

good conscience; at last he will not dare to touch water if more than usually sweet and pure. In fine, he will come to this, that he will deem it criminal to trample on a straw lying in his way.[28]

The second danger is an immoderate use of earthly things amounting to licentious self-indulgence.

> Many are so devoted to luxury in all their senses, that their mind lies buried: many are so delighted with marble, gold, and pictures, that they become marble-hearted—are changed as it were into metal, and made like painted figures. The kitchen, with its savoury smells, so engrosses them that they have no spiritual savour.[29]

Positively, although "the liberty of the Christian in external matters is not to be tied down to a strict rule," there are two laws governing the Christian's use and enjoyment of earthly things.[30] One is that he use the world as not abusing it, as 1 Corinthians 7:29-31 teaches. This is a use that does not involve making too much of the world, so that the world and its things divert the Christian from seeking the heavenly life. The Christian will avoid gluttony, excessive drinking, ostentatious dress, pride, and luxury.

Calvin was especially fearful of luxury in the life of one professing to be a disciple of Christ. Although advocating the middle way between ascetic self-denial and licentious self-indulgence, Calvin exhorted a moderation that sins more on the side of the former than of the latter: "We wish men would follow a moderation closer to abstinence than to luxury."[31]

The second law directing the Christian's use of earthly things is that he bear poverty peaceably and patiently.

Implied by these two laws is a third law. Live earthly life using and enjoying the creatures in the consciousness that we are stewards of these things. For our use of earthly things, we must one day give account. "We must, therefore, administer them as if we constantly heard the words sounding in our ears, 'Give an account of your stewardship.'"[32]

Sixth, and finally, the New Testament patterns the

Christian life by requiring that the Christian must view and occupy his place in everyday life as a divine calling—a "vocation." Calvin spoke of one's "mode of life." He referred to one's earthly station, or job. Viewing his job as a calling, the Christian will not rashly and restlessly abandon it for another. He will patiently bear whatever "inconveniences, cares, uneasiness, and anxiety" attend his "mode of life," "persuaded that God has laid on the burden."[33]

Viewing our station, no matter how lowly, as a divine calling "will afford admirable consolation, that in following your proper calling, no work will be so mean and sordid as not to have a splendour and value in the eye of God."[34]

20

Calvin's Liturgy

Robert Decker

JOHN CALVIN CONDEMNED THE MASS OF ROMAN Catholicism in no uncertain terms. "Of all the idols, he knew none so grotesque as that in which the priest called down Christ into his hands by 'magical mumblings' and offered him anew on the sacrificial altar, while the people looked on in 'stupid amazement.'"[1] Calvin proceeded to formulate his ideas on worship (liturgy) by basing them on the clear warrant of Scripture and appealing to the invariable custom of the ancient church.[2] The reformer concluded, "No assembly of the church should be held without the Word being preached, prayers being offered, the Lord's Supper administered, and alms given."[3]

Calvin's earliest efforts at reforming the worship of the church appeared in the 1536 edition of his *Institutes*:

> As far as the Sacred Supper is concerned, it could have been administered most becomingly if it were set before the church very often, and at least once a week. First, then, it should begin with public prayers. After this a sermon should be given. Then, when bread and wine have been placed on the Table, the minister should repeat the words of institution of the Supper. Next he should recite the promises which were left to us in it; at the same time, he should excommunicate all those who are debarred from it by the Lord's prohibition. Afterward, he should pray that the Lord, with the kindness wherewith he has bestowed this sacred food upon us, also teach and form us to

receive it with faith and thankfulness of heart, and, inasmuch as we are not so of ourselves, by his mercy make us worthy of such a feast. But here, either psalms should be sung, or something should be read, and in becoming order the believers should partake of the most holy banquet, the ministers breaking the bread and giving the cup. When the Supper is finished, there should be an exhortation to sincere faith and confession of faith, to love and behavior worthy of Christians. At the last, thanks should be given, and praises sung to God. When these things are ended, the church should be dismissed in peace.[4]

Calvin never deviated from these ideas, but only expanded on them in the final edition of the *Institutes*. Notice, Calvin insisted on the frequent celebration of the Lord's supper. He wanted it to be celebrated every Lord's day. During Calvin's first pastorate in Geneva, he and Farel proposed in a document titled "Articles Concerning the Organization of the Church and of Worship at Geneva" that the church would be edified by two means especially, the frequent celebration of the Lord's supper and the exercise of discipline. Because of the "frailty of the people," the reformers compromised on a schedule of monthly communion. Later, in 1541, when Calvin returned to Geneva, he attempted to introduce the liturgy he used in Strasbourg. Calvin again attempted to introduce weekly communion, believing there was "nothing more useful to the church than the Lord's Supper. God himself, Calvin believed, added the supper to his word and, therefore, it was a perilous matter to separate them." The council of Geneva, much to Calvin's dismay, insisted upon a quarterly celebration of the Lord's supper. Calvin continued to express his dissatisfaction, declaring as late as 1561, "Our custom is defective."[5]

As is evident from his statement in the *Institutes* of 1536, Calvin's communion liturgy contained four fundamental elements. These elements, the Protestant Reformed reader will recognize, are retained intact in the Form for the Administration of the Lord's Supper.[6] They are: rehearsal of the Lord's institution as the warrant of the sacrament; proclamation of the Lord's promises which relate to his ordi-

Calvin's Liturgy

nance and supply meaning and reality to its signs; excommunication of obdurate sinners; and stress upon worthy participation in the sacrament and holiness of life.

With a couple of exceptions, only the Psalms were sung, and that too without instrumental accompaniment. Concerning instruments Calvin believed "that they formed part of that system of training under the law to which the Church was subjected in its infancy" and, "nor should we foolishly imitate a practice which was intended only for God's ancient people."[7] Incidentally, we are grateful that Calvin's view on this matter did not prevail in the Dutch Reformed tradition.

Calvin's order of worship began with the minister's speaking the majestic words, "Our help is in the name of the Lord, who made heaven and earth. Amen." This was followed by a prayer of confession. This was a brief form prayer read by the minister while the congregation knelt.[8] This was followed by the minister's reading some scriptural promises of forgiveness, after which the minister pronounced the absolution,

> Let each one of you acknowledge himself truly a sinner, humbling himself before God, and believe that the heavenly Father desires to be gracious to him in Jesus Christ. To all who in this manner repent and seek Jesus Christ for their salvation, I declare absolution in the name of the Father, the Son, and the Holy Spirit. Amen.[9]

The absolution was not used in Geneva. After the confession of sin the congregation rose to sing the Ten Commandments as a guide for the grateful obedience of the forgiven Christian.

During the singing the minister left the table for the pulpit. There he prepared for the reading of Scripture and preaching by offering a prayer for illumination. This and the prayer of application after the sermon were the only "free" prayers in Calvin's liturgy. All the other prayers were form prayers. And, even for these two free prayers, Calvin offered the ministers several models.[10] After the prayer of application, the minister offered the congregational prayer. This prayer

151

concluded with the Lord's prayer, which in some congregations was sung by the congregation.

Then, the congregation rose to sing the Apostles' Creed. At this point the congregation was dismissed with the benediction of Aaron based on Numbers 6:24-26, "The LORD bless you and keep you; The LORD make his face to shine upon you, and be gracious to you, the LORD lift up his countenance upon you and give you peace," and with a word about alms, "Remember Jesus Christ in his little ones."[10]

In Geneva, on the four Sundays when the Lord's supper was celebrated, it occurred after the sermon. When the Lord's supper was finished, and before the benediction was pronounced, the congregation sang the song of Simeon, "Lord, now lettest thou thy servant depart in peace...For mine eyes have seen thy salvation" (Luke 2:29, 30).[11]

Calvin's principles of liturgy and the essentials of his order of worship remain in use for the members of the Protestant Reformed Churches. There are some differences in the worship services. For example, we do not kneel to pray, we do not sing either the Apostles' Creed or the Ten Commandments, we do not sing the song of Simeon after the Lord's supper, we do not have an absolution pronounced to the congregation, we have some form prayers but not nearly as many as did Calvin, and we use instrumental accompaniment in the singing of the Psalms. And certainly the Protestant Reformed Churches, with Calvin, make every effort to base worship on the "clear warrant of Scripture," appealing to the invariable "custom of the ancient church."[12]

May God grant us grace to continue in this so that we worship him who is Spirit, "in spirit and in truth" (John 4:24).

21

Worship the Lord in Psalms

Herman Hanko

Psalm Singing and Reformation

WHENEVER GOD BROUGHT REFORMATION TO THE CHURCH of Jesus Christ, a return to Psalm singing was a part of it. This ought not to surprise us. It lies in the nature of reformation.

True reformation in the church always has certain distinguishing characteristics, one of which is a return to what Jeremiah called "the old paths" (Jer. 6:16). Reformation is a return to these old paths in doctrine, church government, and liturgy. Any movement in the church that lacks this characteristic cannot properly be designated church reformation.

The singing of the Psalms characterized the church's worship in its early new-dispensational history. This is not surprising, for the Psalms were God's gift to the church precisely for singing, and the Psalm bundle was all the church had. Two things are important here: the church sang, and the church sang the Psalms.

Gradually the Roman Catholic Church drifted away from congregational singing and from Psalm singing. Congregational singing was replaced by choirs. Again, that such a thing should happen is not surprising, for the Roman Catholic Church denied the priesthood of all believers, that is, the church denied that the people of God possessed the

The Sixteenth-Century Reformation of the Church

Spirit. Paul makes it clear that one must be filled with the Spirit in order to sing: "Be filled with the Spirit; speaking to yourselves in psalms" (Eph. 5:18, 19). It is not even so surprising that the Roman Catholic Church lost the Psalms, for the Psalms, if sung in the church, will keep the church on the path of the truth. Romish theology no longer found expression in the Psalms, so Rome invented songs to express its erroneous doctrines.

There is a reciprocal relation between heresy in the church and a drift from Psalm singing. Certainly, other factors enter when a church loses the truth. But surely one factor is the loss of Psalm singing. It is a fact that in post-Reformation times heresy was sung into the church. But, the relation is reciprocal. A church that drifts from the truth finds the Psalms an inadequate vehicle to express her lust for wrong doctrines.

The Reformation was a return to the old paths: the old paths of the doctrines of free and sovereign grace, the old paths of biblical church government, and the old paths of worship in which the congregation sang Psalms. Calvin, almost from the outset of his work in Geneva, insisted on congregational singing of Psalms. One author goes so far as to say that congregational singing was "one of the four foundations for the reform of the church."[1] He goes on to say: "Calvin placed singing at the heart of his theology of the Church. The reason is not far to seek. To put it with the utmost simplicity: The Church is the place where the gospel is preached; gospel is good news; good news makes people happy; happy people sing."[2]

So it has been throughout post-Reformation history. In the decline of the state church in the Netherlands, choirs were introduced and hymns were sung. In the Afscheiding, led by Hendrik De Cock in 1834, the church returned to congregational singing of the Psalms. In the years prior to 1857, the Reformed Church of America let choirs do part of the singing and all sang hymns. When the Christian Reformed Church began, those saints returned to Psalm singing. In the course of time, the Christian Reformed

Church drifted from her Psalm-singing heritage and thought choirs would be nice. In 1924 the Protestant Reformed Churches returned to congregational singing of the Psalms. In every case it was a part of church reformation. And church reformation always included a return to Psalm singing.

Those who agitate for the introduction of hymns and choirs in the church or tolerate such innovations ought to remember that such innovations always have been a part of departure from the faith.

Psalms and Worship

It is not our purpose to argue in detail the biblical grounds for congregational singing of Psalms. A great deal of literature has been written on the subject, and the interested reader can study the arguments for himself.

A few aspects to this question are, however, worthwhile to consider.

It is a distinctive and emphatic teaching of the Scriptures that the congregation worships. This is what the most important part of keeping the Sabbath day is all about. The members of the congregation of Jesus Christ come together to worship God. They are, on the wings of worship, transported into God's dwelling place in the heavens. In God's presence they worship God. There are different aspects of that worship. In some parts of the worship, the minister leads the congregation in her speech to God—as in the public prayers. In some parts of worship the congregation listens attentively in worship as God speaks to the saints—as in the preaching. In some parts of the worship the congregation actively and on her own engages in worship—as in the singing. Suddenly the minister is only a part of the congregation. Overwhelmed by the wonder of being in God's presence, the congregation joins in speaking to God—in singing. It is the only opportunity for the congregation so to speak.

The Sixteenth-Century Reformation of the Church

This must not be taken from her. Choirs take it away. Choirs are for show, for entertainment, even for edifying. This may be done in programs, but choirs may not steal from the congregation what is her own. A congregation ought to be jealous of this part of her worship and refuse to allow any choir or soloist to steal her own worship.

That the congregation sings is so crucial because the congregation worships in the office of believer. Are only soloists able to worship? Are only choirs able to worship? Cannot God's people worship? Rome denied that God's people were themselves the prophets, priests, and kings who know the Lord, can speak to him, and can rule in his name. The people of God function in the office of believer because they have the Spirit. "Be filled with the Spirit...singing and making melody in your heart to the Lord" (Eph. 5:18, 19).

Many powerful arguments have been set forward by others in defense of exclusive Psalmody. Psalm singing is biblical. Psalm singing is the heritage of the Reformation. Psalm singing is done by the church that is determined to remain faithful to the Reformation. And saints in apostatizing churches, eager to return to the heritage of the Reformation and to walk again in the old paths, throw out the hymns and return to the Psalms.

The point that needs emphasis here is a striking difference between Psalms and most hymns. It is characteristic of most (though not all) hymns that they are either anthropocentric or wrongly Christocentric. That is, they concentrate in man—man's experiences, man's importance—or they concentrate in a Christ who is a friend in some sloppy, sentimental way but is far from the eternal Son of God through whom God reveals himself.

The difference between Psalms and hymns is a crucial difference between apostasy in a church (accompanied by choirs and hymn singing) and reformation in a church (accompanied by congregational Psalm singing).

The theocentric character of the Psalms is exactly comparable to the one crucial issue that always necessitates reformation: the issue between sovereign and particular grace and salvation by human merit and works. It is a striking fact of history that the times when the truths of sovereign and particular grace were strongly and consistently maintained were few and far between, but when these times were present, they were times of church reformation: the reformation of Calvin and Luther over against Rome; the great Synod of Dordt in a death struggle with Arminianism; the truths of sovereign and particular grace in De Cock over against the humanism of the state church; the struggle to defend particular grace over against those who were determined to make it "common."

Hymn singing is, all too often, singing silly songs about man or sloppy songs about Christ. They go along with the constant drift in the church towards Pelagianism and its harlot sister, Arminianism. The robust, powerful, weighty, theocentric Psalms belong to the mighty battle in defense of sovereign and particular grace.

The Psalms and the Christian

The two crucial New Testament passages that enjoin on the congregation of Christ to sing Psalms in worship (Eph. 5:18, 19; Col. 3:16) have some interesting things to say about these Psalms in connection with her singing.

One of them is that singing comes by being filled with the Spirit and by possessing the indwelling of the word of Christ. Those two expressions really mean the same thing, for we have the word of Christ by means of Christ's Spirit.

Christ's Spirit inspired the word of Christ and caused it to be written in the Scriptures. Christ's Spirit puts that word in our hearts, that same inspired word of the Scriptures, so that it becomes our own confession. When Christ's Spirit puts Christ's word in our hearts, then and then only are we able to sing.

This is a powerful and unassailable argument for exclusive Psalmody, but it is also a striking description of what singing ought to be. Some have argued that the singing itself is not important, only the words sung. One may bellow or roar, whisper or mutter, as long as he concentrates on the words. Calvin tended to be suspicious of beautiful singing lest it detract from the words.

The words are indeed the important thing. But the singing is also important. One can express things in music which can be expressed in no other way. We do not sing too well here upon earth, for our singing voices are rather poor. But in heaven the singing too will count. And singing counts now. God has given marvelous gifts in music. The tune, the harmony, the cadence, the poetry, the rhythm, the tempo—all make singing what it truly ought to be. When words and music are perfectly fitted and when the church sings, then God's truth is expressed in ways which only music can accomplish.

The Psalms are so crucially important because the Psalms are that unique book in Scripture which gives us God's own biography of the Christian life. It is all there—from the hand of God. There you will find our only comfort in life and in death, for time and for eternity, for body and for soul: "Whom have I in heaven but thee?" (Ps. 73:25). There you will find that this comfort is ours by way of knowledge of misery: "Against thee, thee only, have I sinned" (Ps. 51:4). There you will find all the truths of deliverance through Christ from his suffering throughout his life to his cross (Ps. 22), resurrection (Ps. 16), ascension (Ps. 68), and exaltation (Ps. 2, 72, 110). There you will find gratitude—gratitude in prayer (Ps. 5) and gratitude in an obedient walk according to God's law (Ps. 119). It is all there: the sufferings, the trials, the temptations, the heartaches, the agony, the pain; but also the joy, the aching wonder of fellowship with God, the awe of a creation singing its doxologies, the quiet serenity of a soul brought in from stormy seas to the quiet calm of the harbor.

It is God's biography of us, a spiritual biography in which every line brings a response, every word an echo, every melody a rush of feeling. We need the Psalms. Hymns have their own experiences of life, but they are man's interpretation and so often are wrong in all sorts of ways. In the Psalms we have God's biography. Then we understand our life as it ought to be understood.

A Reformed church of the Reformation is a church where the congregation of Jesus Christ sings the Psalms.

> That the Psalms in depth of spiritual process by far transcend that which afterwards presented itself as church song, or endeavored to place itself above the Psalms.
>
> That the hymns almost nowhere insinuated themselves into the churches, but they soon revealed the inclination first to replace the Psalms, and afterwards to put them aside.
>
> That in the Psalms resounds the abiding, eternal keynote of the godly mind, while all hymns bear a temporal character, stamping the one-sided conception of the moment in the church of God.
>
> That the hymn almost everywhere has led to all kinds of choir-singing, while the congregation finally fell silent.
>
> That in the struggle between hymn and Psalm, the indifferent in the congregation all took part against the Psalm and for the hymn, while the godly more and more chose for the Psalm and against the hymn.[3]

22

Calvin's Doctrine of Predestination, or Magnifying God's Grace by Double Predestination

Charles Terpstra

───•◦•───

> We shall never be clearly persuaded, as we ought to be, that our salvation flows from the wellspring of God's free mercy until we come to know his eternal election, which illumines God's grace by this contrast: that he does not indiscriminately adopt all into the hope of salvation but gives to some what he denies to others.[1]
>
> Dearly beloved brethren, we must not be amazed if the article of the everlasting predestination to God, be so assaulted and fought against by Satan's maintainers, seeing it is the foundation of our salvation, and also serveth for the better magnifying of the free goodness of God towards us.[2]

A DESCRIPTION OF THE TEACHINGS OF JOHN CALVIN CANNOT be given without including his doctrine of predestination. This truth is fundamental to his theology, flowing throughout it like a crystal-clear brook. We do not refer merely to the doctrine of general predestination, that is, that God sovereignly predestines all things that take place in time and history. This too Calvin taught. Rather we limit ourselves to God's sovereign predestination of his rational, moral creatures, in particular, man. For this is the doctrine so critical to Calvin's Calvinism—still today—but which also comes with so much criticism and controversy.

Calvin's Doctrine of Predestination

Controversy has long surrounded Calvin's doctrine of predestination. Not only were there those in his day who ridiculed his teaching on predestination, but also today theologians argue over the nature of his doctrine and over the place that predestination had in Calvin's theology. For one thing, some have argued that predestination was not the center of his teaching as others had held.[3] Others have claimed that Calvin's doctrine of predestination underwent a significant change following his death. They argue that Theodore Beza, Calvin's successor in Geneva, changed Calvin's doctrine from a warm, biblical presentation to a coldly logical and rationalistic teaching.[4] Then too, there is the controversy involving the place where Calvin dealt with predestination in his theology. Much is made of the fact that he did not treat election and reprobation in connection with the doctrine of God (theology, as was done later in Reformed theology), but in connection with the doctrine of the church (ecclesiology) and the doctrine of salvation (soteriology). This is supposed to indicate that Calvin's doctrine of election and reprobation was not as dominant and strong as in later Calvinism. But this is simply not true, as Calvin's treatment of the doctrine in these places demonstrates. Where he decided to deal with God's predestination did not weaken the doctrine in the least.

But whatever one's view on these issues may be, one thing is certain and all sincere historians and theologians acknowledge that Calvin plainly and powerfully taught God's predestination of mankind, both election and reprobation. He taught it from the beginning of his public ministry, and he continued to develop and clarify it throughout his lifetime. The truth of double predestination is found in the first edition of Calvin's *Institutes* (1536). There he writes, in connection with the doctrine of the church, that the "holy catholic church" is "the whole number of the elect."[5] And a few paragraphs later he states,

> Consequently, the Lord, when he calls his own, justifies and glorifies his own, is declaring nothing but his eternal election, by which he

had destined them to this end before they were born. Therefore no one will enter into the glory of the Heavenly Kingdom, who has not been called in this manner, and justified, seeing that without any exception the Lord in this manner sets forth and manifests his election in all men whom he has chosen.[6]

In subsequent editions of the *Institutes* (1539, 1554, and 1559) Calvin gave the truth of predestination more and more room, as Wendel points out.[7] In that final edition we find Calvin's fullest and finest exposition of the doctrine, as it covers four chapters in the third book, sixty-seven pages in the McNeill/Battles edition.[8] Here the reader will find all the classic aspects of the doctrine treated: God's absolute sovereignty in electing his people and in rejecting all others of the human race; the unconditional nature of God's sovereign choice (without regard to foreknown character or works, as in Jacob and Esau, Romans 9:11); the sovereign mercy and justice of God revealed in the two-sided decree (mercy to the elect, justice to the reprobate); the Christ-centered focus of God's election, as he chose his people in his Son and prepared all their salvation in him and him alone; the unchangeable and effectual character of God's decree, such that the salvation of the elect is absolutely secure, while the damnation of the reprobate is equally sure. To give just a sampling from this edition, this is how Calvin defines predestination at the beginning of his treatment:

> We call predestination God's eternal decree, by which he determined with himself what he willed to become of each man. For all are not created in equal condition; rather, eternal life is foreordained for some, eternal damnation for others. Therefore, as any man has been created to one or the other of these ends, we speak of him as predestined to life or to death.[9]

It is striking and interesting that Calvin also included the doctrine of double predestination in his catechism for the church in Geneva, one published in 1537 especially for the instruction of the youth of that city.[10] In it he tied the doctrine of double predestination not only to the doctrine of the church, as in the early edition of the *Institutes*, but also to the twofold effect of the preaching of the gospel. There he writes,

> The seed of the Word of God takes root and grows fruitful only in those whom the Lord, by his eternal election, has predestined to be his children and heirs of the heavenly kingdom. To all others who, by the same counsel of God before the constitution of the world, are reprobate, the clear and evident preaching of the truth can be nothing else but an odour of death in death.[11]

Calvin's clear teaching on the truth of sovereign predestination can be traced first of all to the fact that he was preeminently a biblical theologian. We know that Calvin was also a great systematizer of the faith of the church, and that he applied those skills in laying out the truth of God's sovereign predestination. That is evident from his treatment of it in his *Institutes*. But he taught and systematized only what he found in the sacred Scriptures. Calvin preached and wrote so much about predestination precisely because he based all he did on the word of God, where that truth is revealed throughout. As he worked with the Bible, whether it was Genesis (see *Sermons on Election and Reprobation*) or Romans (see his commentary on this book), the truth of sovereign predestination was clearly revealed to him. Through the power of the word it became the convicting belief of his own heart, such that he felt compelled to preach it, teach it, and defend it with pulpit and pen. In fact, at the beginning of his treatment of this doctrine in the 1559 *Institutes*, Calvin criticized those who wanted to keep predestination "buried," that is, avoided and suppressed because it was too deep a doctrine. He had in mind, among others, the Lutheran theologian Melanchthon, and he appealed to the Scriptures to defend teaching predestination to the church:

> Therefore, to hold to a proper limit in this regard also, we shall have to turn back to the Word of the Lord, in which we have a sure rule for the understanding. For Scripture is the school of the Holy Spirit, in which, as nothing is omitted that is both necessary and useful to

know, so nothing is taught but what is expedient to know. Therefore we must guard against depriving believers of anything disclosed about predestination in Scripture, lest we seem either wickedly to defraud them of the blessing of their God or to accuse and scoff at the Holy Spirit for having published what it is in any way profitable to suppress.[12]

Another factor in Calvin's strong teaching on predestination was his passion for the glory of God in the sovereignty of his grace. As the two quotes at the beginning of this chapter show, Calvin believed that no doctrine serves more to bring out the greatness and glory of God's sovereign grace than the truth of his eternal election of his people in Jesus Christ. His writings state this repeatedly and consistently. Calvin was convinced that the most powerful way to refute the heresy of free will and all salvation by the work of man is to uphold the doctrine that God has sovereignly chosen his people to salvation from all eternity and included in that election all the means unto and blessings of that salvation. When salvation is grounded in God's sovereign will, the will of man is put in its proper place. And, of course, this is the answer to all free-willism yet today. The contemporary Reformed church must continue to uphold (return to upholding!) the doctrine of God's sovereign predestination, or she will cave in to the errors of free will.

Thus, too, Calvin's doctrine of predestination was developed and refined in the fires of spiritual battle. This is the third factor in his uncompromising exposition of the truth concerning election and reprobation. As today the doctrine of sovereign predestination is hated and attacked, so it was in Calvin's time also. He responded to two attackers of the truth of predestination. First of all, there was the Roman Catholic divine Albertus Pighius, who promoted salvation by the free will of man and predestination on the condition of foreknowledge. Calvin replied to him in 1543 and 1552, setting forth God's sovereign election as the answer to all attempts to have man contribute to his salvation. Second, Calvin did battle against Jerome Bolsec, a renegade and radical Protestant who despised predestination as "godless and blasphemous."[13] Calvin took up the pen against him in two documents. One is the Consensus of Geneva (1552), which is "an elaborate theological argument for the doctrine of absolute predestination, as the only solid ground of comfort to the believer."[14] The other is a treatise entitled "Of the Eternal Predestination of God" (1552), now published in *Calvin's Calvinism*.[15] Here too is his mature doctrine laid out, made sharp and strong by the attacks of the enemy. It is a marvelous defense of sovereign grace through a defense of God's sovereignty in predestination. (We urge the reader to read this treatise!)

Calvin was warm and pastoral in teaching this truth to the saints of God. He taught that the believer can and must receive the assurance and comfort of his election. For this truth makes his salvation absolutely safe and secure. Yet this certainty of one's election is not to be severed from Christ and faith in him. And so, where he ties election to Christ, this is what he writes:

> If we seek salvation, life, and the immortality of the Heavenly Kingdom, then there is no other to whom we may flee, seeing that he [Christ] alone is the fountain of life, the anchor of salvation, and the heir of the Kingdom of Heaven. Now what is the purpose of election but that we, adopted as sons by our Heavenly Father, may obtain salvation and immortality by his favor?...But if we have been chosen in him, we shall not find the assurance of our election in ourselves; and not even in God the Father, if we conceive him as severed from his Son. Christ, then, is the mirror wherein we must, and without self deception may, contemplate our own election. For since it is into his body the Father has destined those to be engrafted whom he has willed from eternity to be his own, that he may hold as sons all whom he acknowledges to be among his members, we have a sufficiently clear and firm testimony that we have been inscribed in the book of life (cf. Rev. 21:27) if we are in communion with Christ.[16]

May we find our own blessed assurance of election to salvation in Christ in this way.

23

An Eschatology of Grace

David J. Engelsma

Someone might doubt whether the Reformation made any distinctive contribution to the doctrine of the last things. That the Reformation recovered the gospel of grace and, in connection with this, the sole authority of Holy Scripture is well known. But did the Reformation say anything distinctive about the last things? Did it do much with eschatology at all? Does it not betray the Reformation's lack of interest in the last things that both Luther and Calvin neglected, indeed refused, to write a commentary on the book of Revelation?

To be sure, there was the rejection of purgatory. That was definitely important for eschatology. But other than this, did the Reformation really influence the church's doctrine of the last things?

To all which, the reply is: "Do you, as a Reformed believer, confidently expect to be with Christ at the moment of your death? Do you look forward, without fear, to the coming of Christ as judge in the final judgment? And is this assurance concerning the future your own in a personal, experiential way—the way of heartfelt, living faith in the promise of God?"

You owe this hope (for this is what the positive answer to the questions is) to the Reformation.

The Reformation set the biblical truths of the last things,

particularly the second coming of Christ for judgment and the death of the believer, in the joyful light of the gospel of grace. This was a radical reformation of the church's teaching on the last things.

Day of Wrath, Day of Mourning

The medieval church had plunged eschatology into the gloomy shadows of its gospel of salvation by the will, works, and worth of man. It taught the people to view their death and the coming of Christ for judgment as divine reckoning on the basis of their own works and worthiness.

This was an eschatology of terror.

It terrified the people. The attitude of the people toward the Day of Christ was that of the popular hymn, "*Dies irae, dies illa*" ("Day of wrath, day of mourning"). The paintings of the Middle Ages vividly portrayed the terrifying eschatology of a gospel of works. A fearsome Christ descends upon the cowering people.

In no small degree, this explains the popularity of the cult of Mary in the developing Roman church. Representing a god of works and merit, Jesus Christ was frightening to the members of the church. Mary, on the other hand, was seen (and preached up) as a sinner's only hope—another gross insult to Jesus Christ, who "hath loved us, and hath given himself for us" (Eph. 5:2).

Before Luther's conversion, his attitude toward death and the judgment was typical. The thunderstorm near Stotternheim not only terrified him with the prospect of death but also drew from him the vow to become a monk. His fear of death was rooted in the notion that only his own works and worth could satisfy a wrathful God. In the monastery, he dreaded judgment and judge with the result that he intensified his feverish efforts to earn acquittal.

The whole of eschatology was a doctrine of damnation and dread. The cause was the false gospel of righteousness by man's own works.

Day of Grace, Day of Laughter

The gospel-truth of justification by faith alone thoroughly revised eschatology. The basis of the final judgment will not be the sinner's own works and worth on account of his free will, but only the perfect work of Jesus Christ on the sinner's behalf. In the final judgment, the lifelong obedience and atoning death of Jesus Christ will be imputed to the sinner through the faith that God gives him. Indeed, the decisive verdict has already been uttered: the "not guilty" of the gospel, heard by faith. There is nothing, absolutely nothing, for the believing sinner to fear in the coming of Christ for judgment.

On the contrary, there is everything to anticipate!

The judge comes to vindicate the righteous believer publicly, before the world. The judgment will finally bestow the reward of grace, so eagerly desired throughout the burdened and afflicted pilgrimage of the godly: eternal life and glory of soul and body in a renewed creation. And for the enjoyment of both public vindication in the judgment and everlasting bliss as the outcome of the judgment, the body of the elect believer will be raised from the grave into immortal life.

Who would not long for the Day of Christ as the day of grace, the day of laughter? Luther called the day of Christ's coming "the most happy Last Day."[1]

The church of the Reformation could again pray, "Come, Lord Jesus" (Rev. 22:20).

The good hope of gracious salvation extends to the believing sinner's death. The gospel of grace dispels the nightmare of purgatory, which Luther, in the Smalcald Articles, called "vermin," the "poison of manifold idolatries," and an "illusion of the devil."[2] How can there be any remaining torment of punishment for one in whose stead Christ died with his all-sufficient death as the gift of a gracious God? The Christian can again face death with calm confidence, indeed desire death, as does the apostle in Philippians 1:21-24. Grace compels the king of terrors to become the believer's helpful servant.

An Eschatology of Grace

The effect of the gospel upon eschatology is reflected in the change of Luther's attitude toward death. Whereas under the malign influence of the gospel of works he had been terrified at death, as a believer in a gracious God he welcomed death.

> We must accustom and discipline ourselves to despise death in faith and to regard it as a deep, strong, and sweet sleep. We must consider the coffin as nothing more than the bosom of our Lord, or paradise, the grave as nothing more than a downy bed on which to lay ourselves...Death and grave mean nothing more than that God neatly lays you as a child in his cradle or soft little bed where you sweetly sleep until the day of judgment.[3]

Luther prayed, "Help us not to fear but to desire death." He confessed, "We should be happy to be dead and desire to die."[4]

Viewing the death of the believer in the light of the grace of salvation in Christ, Calvin rejected the doctrine of soul-sleep. This was the purpose of his first theological work, *Psychopannychia*, dating from 1534. For Calvin, the teaching that the soul of the believer falls asleep at death is a miserable error because it implies disruption of our communion with Christ. It sins against grace.[5]

But we must not suppose that biblical eschatology in the light of grace only enables us to die in peace and to await the coming of Christ without fear. It also empowers us to live. The gospel of works paralyzes the guilty sinner. Or it drives him to work with the motive and demeanor of a slave. The gospel of grace moves the justified sinner to work, with grateful love, in the hope of Christ's coming.

In the hope of Christ's coming!

Not only did the Reformation put all of eschatology under the sign of grace, but it also made eschatology, that is, the second coming of Christ, the goal of the life of the Christian and of the history of the church. Not this life with its trinkets and pleasures, not the dream-world of an earthly millennium, but the resurrection of the body at the coming of Christ must be the one, lively, steady, intense purpose of every Christian and of the church.

John Calvin gave sharpest expression to this practical aspect of biblical eschatology in that section of his *Institutes* where he treated eschatology: "He alone has fully profited in the gospel who has accustomed himself to continual meditation upon the blessed resurrection."[6]

This total recasting of eschatology in the light of grace is evident in the Reformation creeds. "What comfort is it to thee that Christ shall come again to judge the quick and the dead?" asks the Heidelberg Catechism in Question 52. This question was unthinkable for the apostatizing church prior to the Reformation, as it is for the Roman Catholic Church today. The answer of every Reformed believer is that he positively "look[s] for" the coming Christ as judge, to "take me with all his chosen ones, to himself, into heavenly joy and glory." The ground of the comfort is indicated: Christ the judge has "before offered himself for me, to the judgment of God, and removed from me all curse."[7] In the same spirit, Article 37 of the Belgic Confession declares with a fervor that the medieval church would have thought madness that Reformed Christians "expect that great day with a most ardent desire."[8]

As for death, the Heidelberg Catechism says that the death of believers "is not a satisfaction for our sin, but only a dying to sins and entering into eternal life."[9] And the Catechism has every believer confessing that "my soul, after this life, shall be immediately taken up to Christ its head."[10]

Dr. Martin, Get Up!

Not to be overlooked in this Reformation-hope for the coming of Christ is the fact that every believer is personally assured that he himself, as one of the justified, shares the hope. Certain later traditions, under the influence of teaching that urges saints to engage in doubtful introspection, devote enormous amounts of time and ink to demonstrating that a few in the church can finally arrive at their own personal assurance. The effect, often, is to spread still more doubt. This is foreign to the Reformation, which simply assumes that every believer will be certain that he shares the hope of the coming of Christ. Faith is both a certain, or assured, knowledge and a hearty confidence. What this faith believes is the gospel of grace. Thus the Spirit works assurance in every believer, so that he is no more terrified at death than he is at the prospect of falling asleep and no more apprehensive of the coming of Christ than he is of the arrival of a dear brother.

The lively, spontaneous, personal assurance of every believer regarding his own death and Christ's coming for him, Luther expressed in a touching way: "We must sleep until He comes and knocks at our little grave and exclaims, 'Dr. Martin, get up!' Then in the twinkling of an eye I shall rise again and will rejoice with him eternally."[11]

But this is a reality only under the gospel of grace.

In the Roman Catholic Church, this is an impossibility, as Rome itself acknowledges. A gospel that bases salvation on man's own will, works, and worth denies to all any certainty of salvation in the face of death and the judgment.

An eschatology of terror!

This same terror characterizes most of Protestantism today. Embracing Rome's basic theology of free will, Arminian evangelicals and fundamentalists put their people in doubt whether they will be saved at Christ's coming.

Other Protestants are showing themselves careless with regard to the comfort in the face of death and judgment that is only possible under the gospel of grace. These are the men who have compromised the Reformation's doctrine of justification by faith alone in the movement called Evangelicals and Catholics Together. These are also the theologians and churches that tolerate the heresy of free will and conditional salvation.

As for us, living and dying in peace is of some importance. We are determined, therefore, to confess the blessed gospel of salvation by grace alone. We are also determined to curse, damn, and repudiate the false gospel of salvation by the will and works of man.

Here we stand!

In eschatology!

Endnotes

Chapter 1

[1] Philip Schaff, *History of the Christian Church* (1910; reprint, Grand Rapids, Mich.: Eerdmans, 1995), 7:116.
[2] Ibid., 7:130.
[3] Ibid., 7:304, 305.

Chapter 2

[1] John Calvin, preface to *Commentary on the Book of Psalms*, trans. James Anderson (n.d.; reprint, Grand Rapids, Mich.: Baker Books, 1998), xl.
[2] Calvin, "Letter to William Farel, from Strasbourg, August 1541," in *Letters, Part 1*, trans. David Constable, in *Selected Works of John Calvin: Tracts and Letters*, ed. Henry Beveridge and Jules Bonnet, (1858; reprint, Grand Rapids, Mich.: Baker Book House, 1983), 4:280, 281. Calvin's "exile" is a long story you ought to read in a good biography of Calvin.
[3] Thea B. Van Halsema, *This Was John Calvin* (1959; reprint, Grand Rapids, Mich.: Baker Books, 1990), 130.
[4] Ibid., 132.
[5] Schaff, *History of the Christian Church*, 8:839.
[6] Van Halsema, *This Was John Calvin*, 213.
[7] Schaff, *History of the Christian Church*, 8:822.

Chapter 3

[1] Karl Holl, *What Did Luther Understand by Religion?* (Philadelphia: Fortress Press, 1977), 4.
[2] Martin Luther, "Letter to Martin Bucer, from Wittenberg, October 14, 1539," in *Letters III*, ed. and trans. Gottfried G. Krodel, in *Luther's Works*, ed. Helmut T. Lehmann (Philadelphia: Fortress Press, 1975), 50:190, 191.

[3] David Steinmetz, *Luther in Context* (Grand Rapids, Mich.: Baker Books, 1995), 85, 86.
[4] John T. McNeill, "Calvin's Efforts toward Consolidation of Protestantism," *The Journal of Religion* (July 1928): 421.
[5] Calvin, "Letter to Bullinger," in *Letters, Part 1*, in *Selected Works of John Calvin*, 4:433.
[6] David Steinmetz, *Calvin in Context* (New York: Oxford University Press, 1995), 172.
[7] Luther, *The Bondage of the Will*, trans. J. I. Packer and O. R. Johnston (London: James Clarke & Co., 1957; reprint, with an introduction by J. I. Packer and O. R. Johnston, Grand Rapids, Mich.: Fleming H. Revell, Baker Book House, 1995), 199, 200.
[8] Ibid., 217.
[9] Ibid., 58, 59.
[10] Karl Holl, *What Did Luther Understand by Religion?* (Philadelphia: Fortress Press, 1977), 106.

Chapter 4

[1] P. Hume Brown, *John Knox: A Biography* (London: Adams and Charles Black, 1895), 1:71.
[2] Ibid., 1:97.
[3] John Knox, *Selected Writings of John Knox: Public Epistles, Treatises, and Expositions to the Year 1559*, ed. Kevin Reed (Dallas: Presbyterian Heritage Publications, 1995), 7.
[4] Brown, *John Knox: A Biography*, 1:76.
[5] Brown, *John Knox: A Biography*, 1:250, 251.
[6] Knox, *Selected Writings*, 316, 317.
[7] Ibid., 16.
[8] Brown, *John Knox: A Biography*, 2:278, 279.
[9] *The New Schaff-Herzog Encyclopedia of Religious Knowledge* (New York: Funk and Wagnalls, 1920), s.v. "Knox, John."
[10] Brown, *John Knox: A Biography*, 2:288.

Chapter 5

[1] Calvin, "Letter to Bullinger, from Geneva, April, 1554," in

Endnotes

Letters, Part 3, trans. Marcus Robert Gilchrist, in *Selected Works of John Calvin: Tracts and Letters*, ed. Henry Beveridge and Jules Bonnet (1858; reprint, Grand Rapids, Mich.: Baker Book House, 1983) 6:37.
[2] T. M'Crie, *The Life of John Knox* (Philadelphia: Presbyterian Board of Publication, 1905), 93.
[3] Ibid., 94.
[4] Ibid., 94, 95.
[5] Calvin, "Letter to William Cecil," in *Letters, Part 4*, trans. Marcus Robert Gilchrist, in *Selected Works of John Calvin: Tracts and Letters*, ed. Henry Beveridge and Jules Bonnet (1858; reprint, Grand Rapids, Mich.: Baker Book House, 1983), 7:47.
[6] Ibid., 48.
[7] Calvin, "Letter to John Knox, from Geneva, June 12, 1555," in *Letters, Part 3, in Selected Works of John Calvin*, 6:189-191. See also Calvin, "Letter to John Knox, from Geneva, April 23, 1561," in *Letters, Part 4, in Selected Works of John Calvin*, 7:183-185.
[8] John Knox, *Works of John Knox* (1854; reprint, Edmonton, Alberta: Still Waters Revival Books, n.d.) 3:201. See also 4:41, 161 and 6:133-135 which show his great respect for Calvin and esteem for Calvin's advice.
[9] Knox, *Works of John Knox*, 4:240.
[10] Calvin, "Letter to John Knox, from Geneva, November 7, 1559," in *Letters, Part 4, in Selected Works of John Calvin*, 7:73, 76. This was written after the one to Cecil (May 1559), in which Calvin expressed anger at Knox. Knox and Calvin had obviously talked this matter out to their mutual satisfaction.
[11] Calvin, "Letter to John Knox, from Geneva, April 23, 1561," in *Letters, Part 4, in Selected Works of John Calvin*, 7:183-185.
[12] Calvin, "Letter to Christopher Goodman, from Geneva, April 23, 1561," in *Letters, Part 4, in Selected Works of John Calvin*, 7:185-186.
[13] Calvin, "Letter to the Earl of Arran, August 1, 1558," in *Letters, Part 3, in Selected Works of John Calvin*, 6:455.

14 Calvin, *Sermons on Election and Reprobation* (1579; reprint, Audubon, N.J.: Old Paths Publications, 1996), xxviii.

Chapter 6

1 Calvin, preface to *Commentary on Psalms*, xxxv-xlix.
2 Ironically, the one who so identified Calvin and who therefore was indirectly responsible for the influential place Calvin received in Geneva, though not himself identified by name, is said by Calvin to have been an individual who subsequently apostatized and returned to the papists (Calvin, preface to *Commentary on Psalms*, xlii, xliii).
3 Calvin, preface to *Commentary on Psalms*, xlii.
4 Philip E. Hughes, ed. and trans., introduction to *The Register of the Company of Pastors of Geneva in the Time of Calvin* (Grand Rapids, Mich.: Eerdmans, 1966), 5.
5 Calvin, preface to *Commentary on Psalms*, xliii.
6 Theodore Beza, *The Life of John Calvin*, ed. and trans. Henry Beveridge (Milwaukie, Ore.: Back Home Industries, 1996), 30.
7 Jacopo Sadoleto, "Letter to the Genevans," *A Reformation Debate*, ed. John C. Olin, trans. Henry Beveridge (Grand Rapids, Mich.: Baker Book House, 1966), 29.
8 Ronald S. Wallace, *Calvin, Geneva, and the Reformation* (Grand Rapids, Mich.: Baker Books, 1998), 24.
9 Calvin, preface to *Commentary on Psalms*, xliv.
10 *The Church Order of the Protestant Reformed Churches*, which is essentially the Church Order of Dordrecht (1618-1619), bears clear evidence of being greatly influenced by Calvin's "Ecclesiastical Ordinances" found in *Register of the Company of Pastors of Geneva*, Philip E. Hughes (Grand Rapids, Mich.: Eerdmans, 1966), 35-49.

Chapter 7

1 Martin Luther, "Against the Roman Papacy, an Institution of the Devil," in *Church and Ministry III*, ed. and trans. Eric W. Gritsch, in *Luther's Works*, ed. Helmut T. Lehmann

Endnotes

(Philadelphia: Fortress Press, 1966), 41:269, 272. See also 263-376.
[2] William Bentley Ball, "Why Can't We Work Together," *Christianity Today* (July 16, 1990): 22-24.
[3] This chapter was originally published October 15, 1990.
[4] Pope John Paul II visited Chicago in 1979.
[5] Canons 9 and 15, Chap. 16 of "On Justification," *Canons and Decrees of the Council of Trent*, trans. Rev. J. Waterworth (Chicago: Christian Symbolic Publication Society, n.d.), 45, 46.
[6] Walter M. Abbott, ed., *The Documents of Vatican II* (New York: America Press, 1966), 117.
[7] Ibid., 43, 81, 96, 91. See also 43-96.
[8] Ibid., 535.
[9] Ibid., 84, 78-85.
[10] Heidelberg Catechism, Q & A 80, in Philip Schaff, ed., *Creeds of Christendom* (1931; reprint, Grand Rapids, Mich.: Baker Books, 1998), 3:335, 336.
[11] Belgic Confession, Art. 29, Schaff, *Creeds of Christendom*, 3:419-421.
[12] Luther, "Against the Roman Papacy," in *Church and Ministry III*, in *Luther's Works*, 41:302.

Chapter 8

[1] Willem Balke, *Calvin and the Anabaptist Radicals*, trans. William Heynen (Grand Rapids, Mich.: Eerdmans, 1981), 2-4. Balke speaks of seven different branches of Anabaptism.
[2] Belgic Confession, Art. 18, Schaff, *Creeds of Christendom*, 3:402, 403.
[3] Some claim that the entire Anabaptist movement began with these men. Others claim that the Wittenburg iconoclasts were the beginning.
[4] Question and Answer 101 of the Heidelberg Catechism was written in answer to the Anabaptists. See Schaff, *Creeds of Christendom*, 3:344.

Chapter 9

[1] John Knox, *A Warning against the Anabaptists* (Dallas, Tex.: Presbyterian Heritage Publications, 1984), 29, 30.
[2] Conrad Grebel, "Letter to Thomas Muntzer," *Spiritual and Anabaptist Writers*, ed. George H. Williams (Philadelphia: Westminster Press, 1957), 81.
[3] Schleitheim Confession, in *Confessions and Catechisms of the Reformation*, ed. Mark Noll (Grand Rapids, Mich.: Baker Books, 1991), 51, 52.
[4] William R. Estep, *The Anabaptist Story*, rev. ed. (Grand Rapids, Mich.: Eerdmans, 1975).
[5] Galen Meyer, "Whitewater Impressions," *The Banner* (Sept. 23, 1991): 8; Phyllis Ten Elshof, "Hundreds Rise to Life Challenge," *The Banner* (Sept. 23, 1991): 23; Galen Meyer, "Ken Medema: Wild and Sanctified," *The Banner* (Sept. 23, 1991): 26.
[6] Henry Danhof and Herman Hoeksema, *Niet Doopersch maar Gereformeerd* (Grand Rapids, Mich.: Grand Rapids Printing, n.d.), 67, 68. Engelsma's translation of the Dutch.
[7] Belgic Confession, Art. 29, Schaff, *Creeds of Christendom*, 3:419-421.

Chapter 10

[1] Benjamin B. Warfield, "Literary History of Calvin's *Institutes*" in Calvin, *Institutes of the Christian Religion*, trans. John Allen (Philadelphia: Presbyterian Board of Christian Education, n.d.), 1:v.
[2] Calvin, *Institutes*, trans. Allen, 1.6.1.
[3] Ibid., 1.7.1.
[4] Ibid., 1.7.1.
[5] Ibid., 1.7.2.
[6] Ibid., 1.7.3.
[7] Ibid., 1.7.4.
[8] Ibid., 1.7.5.
[9] Ibid., 1.8.1.
[10] Ibid., 1.8.2.

Endnotes

[11] Ibid., 1.8.12.
[12] Ibid., 1.8.13.
[13] Ibid., 1.9.1.
[14] Ibid., 1.9.3.

Chapter 11

[1] *The New Schaff-Herzog Encyclopedia of Religious Knowledge* (New York: Funk and Wagnalls, 1909), s.v. "Exegesis or Hermeneutics," 3.5.
[2] Calvin, *Commentary on the Epistles to Timothy, Titus, and Philemon*, trans. William Pringle (Grand Rapids, Mich.: Eerdmans, 1948), 249.
[3] Belgic Confession, Art. 5, Schaff, *Creeds of Christendom*, 3:386, 387.
[4] Schaff, *History of the Christian Church*, 8:104, 105.
[5] Calvin, *Institutes*, trans. Beveridge, 1.13.1.
[6] A. Skevington Wood, *Captive to the Word* (Grand Rapids, Mich.: Eerdmans, 1969), 164.
[7] Ibid., 164, 165.
[8] Ibid., 162.
[9] Ibid., 171, 172.
[10] Luther, "Preface to the Epistles of St. James and St. Jude," in *Word and Sacrament I*, ed. E. Theodore Bachmann, trans. Charles M. Jacobs and E. Theodore Bachmann, in *Luther's Works*, ed. Helmut T. Lehmann (Philadelphia: Muhlenberg Press, 1960), 35:396.
[11] Wood, *Captive to the Word*, 159-161.

Chapter 12

[1] Luther, *The Bondage of the Will*, trans. Packer and Johnston, 40, 41, 58.
[2] Ibid., 123.
[3] Ibid., 123.
[4] Ibid., 124.
[5] Ibid., 124.
[6] Ibid., 125.

[7] Ibid., 73, 74, 124, 125.
[8] Ibid., 74; emphasis added.
[9] Ibid., 240; see also 191, 192.
[10] Ibid., 247
[11] Ibid., 99.
[12] Ibid., 71.
[13] Ibid., 66.
[14] Ibid., 67.
[15] Ibid.
[16] Ibid., 66, 67.
[17] Ibid., 70.
[18] Ibid., 66.

Chapter 13

[1] Luther, "Sermon, Matt. 22:37-39," in *Sermons I*, ed. and trans. John W. Doberstein, in *Luther's Works*, ed. Helmut T. Lehmann (Philadelphia: Muhlenberg Press, 1959), 51:107.
[2] Luther, "Psalm 82," in *Selected Psalms II*, ed. Jaroslav Pelikan, trans. C. M. Jacobs, in *Luther's Works*, ed. Jaroslav Pelikan (St. Louis: Concordia Publishing House, 1956), 13:49.
[3] T. H. L. Parker, *The Oracles of God: An Introduction to the Preaching of John Calvin* (London: Lutterworth Press, 1947), 20.
[4] Wood, *Captive to the Word*, 89.
[5] Luther, "Isaiah 40," in *Lectures on Isaiah 40-66*, ed. Hilton C. Oswald, trans. Herbert J. A. Bouman, in *Luther's Works*, ed. Jaroslav Pelikan (St. Louis: Concordia Publishing House, 1972), 17:8.
[6] Ibid.
[7] Luther, "Psalm 26," in *Selected Psalms I*, ed. Jaroslav Pelikan, trans. Lewis W. Spitz Jr., in *Luther's Works*, ed. Jaroslav Pelikan (St. Louis: Concordia Publishing House, 1955), 12:186.
[8] Luther, "Psalm 2," in Selected *Psalms I*, in *Luther's Works*, 12:43.
[9] Luther, "Sermon on John 6:37," in *Sermons on the Gospel of*

Endnotes

St. John 6-8, ed. Jaroslav Pelikan, trans. Martin H. Bertram, in *Luther's Works*, ed. Jaroslav Pelikan (St. Louis: Concordia Publishing House, 1959), 23:98.

[10] Luther, "Sermon on John 14:10," *Sermons on the Gospel of St. John 14-16*, ed. Jaroslav Pelikan, trans. Martin H. Bertram, in *Luther's Works*, ed. Jaroslav Pelikan (St. Louis: Concordia Publishing House, 1959), 24:66.

[11] Luther, "Psalm 110," in *Selected Psalms II*, in *Luther's Works*, 13:291.

[12] Luther, "Lecture on Genesis 6:3," in *Lectures on Genesis 6-14*, ed. Jaroslav Pelikan, trans. George V. Schick, in *Luther's Works*, ed. Jaroslav Pelikan (St. Louis: Concordia Publishing House, 1960), 2:17.

[13] Luther, "Sermon, Matt. 22:37-39," in *Sermons I*, in *Luther's Works*, 51:111.

[14] Luther, "Lecture on Galatians 3:4," in *Lectures on Galatians*, ed. and trans. Jaroslav Pelikan, in *Luther's Works*, ed. Jaroslav Pelikan (St. Louis: Concordia Publishing House, 1964), 27:249.

[15] Luther, "Psalm 110," in *Selected Psalms II*, in *Luther's Works*, 13:271, 272.

[16] Luther, "Forty-seventh Sermon on the Gospel of St. John," in *Sermons on the Gospel of St. John 1-4*, ed. Jaroslav Pelikan, trans. Martin H. Bertram, in *Luther's Works*, ed. Jaroslav Pelikan (St. Louis: Concordia Publishing House, 1957), 22:483.

[17] Luther, "Isaiah 57," in *Lectures on Isaiah 40-66*, in *Luther's Works*, 17:277.

[18] Luther, *Lectures on Romans*, trans. of *Römerbriefvorlesung*, in *Luther's Works*, Weimar ed. (Philadelphia: Muhlenberg Press, 1961), 56:3, 4. A different translation can be found in the American edition of *Luther's Works*, 25:135, 136.

[19] Luther, "Heidelberg Disputation, 1518," in *Career of the Reformer I*, ed. and trans. Harold J. Grimm, in *Luther's Works*, ed. Helmut T. Lehmann (Philadelphia: Muhlenberg Press, 1957), 31:51.

[20] Luther, "The Freedom of a Christian, 1520," in *Career of the Reformer I*, in *Luther's Works*, 31:364.

[21] Luther, "Isaiah 40," in *Lectures on Isaiah 40-66,* in *Luther's Works,* 17:14.

[22] Luther, "Sermon, Matt. 22:37-39," in *Sermons I,* in *Luther's Works,* 51:112.

[23] Luther, "Lecture on Genesis 13," in *Lectures in Genesis 6-14,* in *Luther's Works,* 2:334.

[24] Luther, "Lecture on Genesis 6:3," in *Lectures in Genesis 6-14,* in *Luther's Works,* 2:18.

Chapter 14

[1] This was written in Latin. A similar, though not identical, defense in German was published in 1521, with the title (translated) *The Defense and Explanation of All the Articles of Dr. Martin Luther Which Were Unjustly Condemned by the Roman Bull.* This is available in English in volume 32 of *Luther's Works.*

[2] E. Gordon Rupp. et al., ed. and trans., *Luther and Erasmus: Free Will and Salvation,* in *Library of Christian Classics* (Philadelphia: Westminster Press, 1969), 17:64.

[3] Luther, "Letter to John Lang, from Wittenberg, March 1, 1517," in *Letters I,* ed. and trans. Gottfried G. Krodel, in *Luther's Works,* ed. Helmut T. Lehmann (Philadelphia: Fortress Press, 1963), 48:40.

[4] Erasmus, "Letter to Luther, from Louvain, May 30, 1519," in *The Correspondence of Erasmus,* trans. R. A. B. Mynors and D. F. S. Thomson (Toronto: University of Toronto Press, 1982), 6:391, 392.

[5] Erasmus, *Diatribe on the Freedom of the Will,* in *Luther and Erasmus: Free Will and Salvation,* ed. and trans. E. Gordon Rupp et al., *Library of Christian Classics* (Philadelphia: Westminster Press, 1969), 17:35-97.

[6] Ibid., 36.

[7] Ibid., 38, 39.

[8] Ibid., 82.

[9] Ibid., 87.

[10] Ibid., 89, 90.

[11] Luther, *The Bondage of the Will*, trans. Henry Cole (Grand Rapids, Mich.: Baker Book House, 1976), section 168.
[12] Ibid., Introduction.
[13] Ibid., section 19.
[14] Ibid., section 7.
[15] Ibid., section 26.
[16] Ibid., section 36.
[17] Ibid., section 47.
[18] Ibid., section 52.
[19] Ibid., section 56.
[20] Ibid., section 58.
[21] Ibid., section 64.
[22] Ibid., section 68.
[23] Ibid., section 69.
[24] Ibid., section 70.
[25] Ibid., section 81.
[26] Ibid., section 94.
[27] Ibid.
[28] Ibid., section 157.
[29] Ibid., section 159.

Chapter 15

[1] Quoted in "Preface to the Complete Edition of Luther's Latin Writings," in *Career of the Reformer IV*, ed. and trans. Lewis W. Spitz, in *Luther's Works*, ed. Helmut T. Lehmann (Philadelphia: Muhlenberg Press, 1960), 34:336, 337. Many of these quotations from Luther's works can also be found in Robin A. Leaver, *Luther on Justification* (St. Louis: Concordia Publishing House, 1975).
[2] Luther, "To Some Pastors of the City of Lübeck, Wittenberg, January 12, 1530," in *Letters II*, ed. and trans. Gottfried G. Krodel, in *Luther's Works*, ed. Helmut T. Lehmann (Philadelphia: Fortress Press, 1972), 49:262, 263.
[3] Witness the publication, signing, and defense in 1994 of the document "Evangelicals and Catholics Together" by a number of leading "evangelicals," which document finds no

essential difference between the Romish and Protestant doctrines of justification.

[4] Luther, "Letter to George Spenlein, Wittenberg, April 8, 1516," in *Letters I*, ed. and trans. Gottfried G. Krodel, in *Luther's Works*, ed. Helmut T. Lehmann (Philadelphia: Fortress Press, 1963), 48:12.

[5] Timothy George, *Theology of the Reformers* (Nashville: Broadman Press, 1988), 71.

[6] Luther, "The Freedom of a Christian, 1520," in *Career of the Reformer I*, in *Luther's Works*, 31:352.

[7] Luther, "The Argument of St. Paul's Epistle to the Galatians," in *Lectures on Galatians*, ed. and trans. Jaroslav Pelikan, in *Luther's Works*, ed. Jaroslav Pelikan (St. Louis: Concordia Publishing House, 1963), 26:9.

[8] By the use of the word "passive," Luther also meant that the faith which unites us to Christ unites us to his suffering (the words "passive" and "passion" are related). Thus, too, justifying faith is far from inactive in that it shares, through union with Christ, in Christ's suffering. That suffering, according to Luther, included not only sharing in Christ's reproach and persecution, but in the agony of dying to sin and being killed by the law.

[9] Luther, "Sermon on John 6:28, 29," in *Sermons on the Gospel of St. John 6-8*, in *Luther's Works*, 23:23.

[10] Luther, "Preface to the Epistle of St. Paul to the Romans," in *Word and Sacrament I*, ed. and trans. E. Theodore Bachmann, trans. Charles M. Jacobs, in *Luther's Works*, ed. Helmut T. Lehmann (Philadelphia: Muhlenberg Press, 1960), 35:370.

[11] Luther, "On Translating: An Open Letter," in *Word and Sacrament I*, in *Luther's Works*, 35:188.

[12] Luther, "Sermon on John 14:6," in *Sermons on the Gospel of St. John 14-16*, in *Luther's Works*, 24:48.

[13] Luther, "Lecture on Galatians 4:9," in *Lectures on Galatians 1-4*, ed. and trans. Jaroslav Pelikan, in *Luther's Works*, ed. Jaroslav Pelikan (St. Louis: Concordia Publishing House, 1963), 26:403, 404.

[14] Luther, "Heidelberg Disputation, Thesis 16," *Luther's*

Works, 31:40. An excellent analysis of the "Heidelberg Disputation" is found in Gerhard O. Forde, *On Being a Theologian of the Cross: Reflections on Luther's Heidelberg Disputation*, 1518 (Grand Rapids, Mich.: Eerdmans, 1997).

[15] Luther, "Theses Concerning Faith and Law, 1535," in *Career of the Reformer IV*, in *Luther's Works*, 34:114.

[16] Gerhard O. Forde, *On Being a Theologian of the Cross*, 62, 63.

[17] Luther, *The Bondage of the Will*, ed. J. I. Packer and O. R. Johnston (London: James Clarke, 1957), 103, 104.

[18] Luther, "Heidelberg Disputation, Thesis 25, 26," *Luther's Works*, 31:40. Quoted in Forde, *On Being a Theologian of the Cross*, 103-110.

[19] Luther, "Sermon on John 15:17-18," in *Sermons on the Gospel of St. John 14-16*, in *Luther's Works*, 24:264, 265.

[20] Leaver, *Luther on Justification*, 81; note 55.

[21] Luther, "Lectures on Hebrews 10," in *Lectures on Titus, Philemon, and Hebrews*, ed. and trans. Walter A. Hansen, in *Luther's Works*, ed. Jaroslav Pelikan (St. Louis: Concordia Publishing, 1968), 29:224.

[22] George, *Theology of the Reformers*, 54.

[23] Luther, "Sermon on the Sum of the Christian Life," in *Sermons I*, in *Luther's Works*, 51:282.

[24] Luther, "Psalm 117," in *Selected Psalms III*, ed. Jaroslav Pelikan, trans. Edward Sittler, in *Luther's Works*, ed. Jaroslav Pelikan (St. Louis: Concordia Publishing, 1958), 14:37, 38.

[25] Luther, *Table Talk*, ed. and trans. Theodore G. Tappert, in *Luther's Works*, ed. Helmut T. Lerhmann (Philadelphia: Fortress Press, 1967), 54:340.

[26] Luther, "Psalm 117," in *Selected Psalms III*, in *Luther's Works*, 14:37, 38.

Chapter 16

[1] Calvin, *Institutes of the Christian Religion*, trans. Henry Beveridge (1845; reprint, 2 vols. in 1, Grand Rapids, Mich.: Eerdmans, 1989), 3.11.2.

[2] Schaff, *History of the Christian Church*, 7:122.

[3] Luther, Smalcald Articles (Part 2, Art. 1), in *The Book of Concord: The Confessions of the Evangelical Lutheran Church*, ed. and trans. Theodore G. Tappert (Philadelphia: Fortress Press, 1959), 292.
[4] Calvin, *Institutes of the Christian Religion*, ed. John T. McNeill, trans. Ford Lewis Battles (Philadelphia: Westminster Press, 1960), 3.11.1.
[5] Calvin, *Institutes*, trans. Beveridge, 3.11.1.
[6] See Augsburg Confession, Art. 4 (Schaff, *Creeds of Christendom*, 3:10); Belgic Confession, Art. 17, 18, 20, 22 (Ibid., 3:402, 403, 405, 407-409); Heidelberg Catechism, Q & A 60, 61 (Ibid., 3:326, 327); Second Helvetic Confession, Chapter 15 (Ibid., 3:862-864); Westminster Confession of Faith, Chapter 11 (Ibid., 3:626-628); French Confession, Art. 18 (Ibid., 3:369, 370).
[7] Chap. 4 of "On Justification," *Canons and Decrees*, 32.
[8] Chap. 7 of "On Justification," *Canons and Decrees*, 34.
[9] Canon 24, Chap. 16 of "On Justification," *Canons and Decrees*, 47.
[10] Chap. 8 of "On Justification," *Canons and Decrees*, 36.
[11] Canon 9, Chap. 16 of "On Justification," *Canons and Decrees*, 45.
[12] Calvin, *Institutes*, trans. Beveridge, 3.11.11.
[13] Ibid., 3.11.21. Calvin uses the word "condition" here to refer to man's legal standing before God.
[14] Ibid., 3.16.1.
[15] Francis Turretin, *Institutes of Elenctic Theology*, ed. James T. Dennison, trans. George Musgrave Griger (Phillipsburg, N.J.: P & R Publishing, 1992), 2:633.

Chapter 17

[1] Loraine Boettner, *Roman Catholicism* (Philadelphia: Presbyterian and Reformed Publishing, 1962), 220.
[2] "Decree Concerning Purgatory," *Canons and Decrees*, 232.
[3] Charles Chiniquy, *Fifty Years in the Church of Rome* (1886; reprint, Grand Rapids, Mich.: Baker Book House, 1958), 48.

Endnotes

Chapter 18

[1] Luther, "The Freedom of a Christian, 1520," in *Career of the Reformer I*, in *Luther's Works*, 31:335.
[2] Calvin, "Reply by John Calvin to Letter by Cardinal Sadolet to the Senate and People of Geneva," in *Tracts, Part 1*, ed. and trans. Henry Beveridge, in *Selected Works of John Calvin: Tracts and Letters*, ed. Henry Beveridge and Jules Bonnet (1844; reprint, Grand Rapids, Mich.: Baker Book House, 1980), 1:49.
[3] Henri Daniel-Rops, *The Protestant Reformation*, trans. Audrey Butler (London: J. M. Dent & Son, 1961), 297.
[4] Luther, "Against the Heavenly Prophets in the Matter of Images and Sacraments, 1525," in *Church and Ministry II*, ed. Conrad Bergendoff, trans. Bernhard Erling and Conrad Bergendoff, in *Luther's Works*, ed. Helmut T. Lehmann (Philadelphia: Muhlenberg Press, 1958), 40:73-223.
[5] Luther, *Table Talk*, in *Luther's Works*, 54:22.
[6] Calvin, *Commentaries on Timothy, Titus, and Philemon*, 154. Emphasis added.
[7] Luther, "Proceedings at Augsburg, 1518," in *Career of the Reformer I*, in *Luther's Works*, 31:257.
[8] Luther, "Sermon on Soberness and Moderation against Gluttony and Drunkenness," in *Sermons I*, in *Luther's Works*, 51:291-299.

Chapter 19

[1] Calvin, *Golden Book of the True Christian Life*, trans. Henry J. Van Andel (Grand Rapids, Mich.: Baker Books, 1952).
[2] Calvin, *Institutes*, trans. Beveridge, 3.6.4.
[3] Ibid.
[4] Ibid., 3.6.1.
[5] Ibid., 3.6.2, 3.
[6] Ibid., 3.7.1.
[7] Ibid.
[8] Ibid.
[9] Ibid., 3.7.4.

[10] Ibid., 3.7.6.
[11] Ibid., 3.7.7.
[12] Ibid., 3.7.8.
[13] Ibid., 3.7.10.
[14] Ibid., 3.8.1.
[15] Ibid.
[16] Ibid., 3.8.7.
[17] Ibid., 3.8.5.
[18] Ibid., 3.8.7.
[19] Ibid., 3.8.3.
[20] Ibid., 3.8.8.
[21] Ibid., 3.9.1.
[22] Ibid., 3.9.2.
[23] Ibid., 3.9.1.
[24] Ibid., 3.9.3.
[25] Ibid., 3.9.5.
[26] Ibid., 3.9.6.
[27] Ibid., 3.10.1.
[28] Ibid., 3.19.7.
[29] Ibid., 3.10.3.
[30] Ibid., 3.10.4.
[31] Calvin, "Concerning Luxury," in Ford Lewis Battles, *Inter-preting John Calvin* (Grand Rapids, Mich.: Baker Books, 1996), 329.
[32] Calvin, *Institutes*, trans. Beveridge, 3.10.5.
[33] Ibid., 3.10.6.
[34] Ibid.

Chapter 20

[1] Bard Thompson, *Liturgies of the Western Church* (New York: New American Library, 1961), 185.
[2] In addition to Thompson's book and the pertinent sections of Calvin's *Institutes*, the reader who wishes to pursue this subject further ought to read James Hastings Nichols, *Corporate Worship in the Reformed Tradition* (Philadelphia: Westminster Press, 1968).
[3] Calvin, *Institutes of the Christian Religion* (1536), trans. Ford

Lewis Battles, rev. ed. (Grand Rapids, Mich.: Eerdmans, 1986), 122, 123.
[4] Thompson, *Liturgies of the Western Church*, 185, 186.
[5] Ibid., 190.
[6] Form for the Administration of the Lord's Supper, *The Psalter with Doctrinal Standards, Liturgy, Church Order, and Added Chorale Section*, rev. ed. (Grand Rapids, Mich.: Eerdmans, 1995), 91-96.
[7] Calvin, *Commentary on the Psalms*, 266, 312.
[8] Nichols, *Corporate Worship*, 41, 42.
[9] Ibid., 43.
[10] Ibid., 51.
[11] Ibid.
[12] Thompson, *Liturgies of the Western Church*, 185.

Chapter 21

[1] T. H. L. Parker, *John Calvin: A Biography* (London: J. M. Dent and Sons, 1975), 87.
[2] Ibid.
[3] Abraham Kuyper, *Onze Eeredienst* (*Our Public Worship*) (Kampen: Kok, 1911), 56. Hanko's translation of the Dutch.

Chapter 22

[1] Calvin, *Institutes*, trans. Battles, 3.21.1.
[2] Calvin, *Sermons on Election and Reprobation*, 305.
[3] François Wendel, *Calvin: The Origins and Development of His Religious Thought*, trans. Philip Mairet (New York: Wm. Collins, 1965; reprint, Grand Rapids, Mich.: Baker Books, 1997), 263.
[4] Alister E. McGrath, *A Life of John Calvin: A Study in the Shaping of Western Culture* (Grand Rapids, Mich.: Baker Books, 1990), 211.
[5] Calvin, *Institutes* (1536), trans. Battles, 58.
[6] Calvin, *Institutes* (1536), trans. Battles, 58, 59.
[7] Wendel, *Calvin: Origins and Development*, 264.
[8] Calvin, *Institutes*, trans. Battles, 920-987.

[9] Ibid., 3.21.5.
[10] Calvin, "Catechism of the Church of Geneva," in *Tracts, Part 2*, ed. and trans. Henry Beveridge, in *Selected Works of John Calvin: Tracts and Letters*, ed. Henry Beveridge and Jules Bonnet (1849; reprint, Grand Rapids, Mich.: Baker Book House, 1980), 2:50. "What is the Church? The body and society of believers whom God hath predestined to eternal life."
[11] Wendel, *Calvin: Origins and Development*, 266.
[12] Calvin, *Institutes*, trans. Battles, 3.21.3.
[13] Schaff, *Creeds of Christendom*, 1:474.
[14] Ibid., 1:475.
[15] Calvin, *Calvin's Calvinism*, trans. Henry Cole (1856; reprint, Grandville, Mich.: Reformed Free Publishing Association, 1987).
[16] Calvin, *Institutes*, trans. Battles, 3.24.5.

Chapter 23

[1] Paul Althaus, *The Theology of Martin Luther* (Philadelphia: Fortress Press, 1966), 420, 421.
[2] Luther, Smalcald Articles (Part 2, Art. 2), in *The Book of Concord*, 294.
[3] Herman Quistorp, *Calvin's Doctrine of the Last Things* (London: Lutterworth Press, 1955), 99, 100.
[4] Althaus, *The Theology of Martin Luther*, 408.
[5] Calvin, "Psychopannychia," in *Tracts, Part 3*, ed. and trans. Henry Beveridge, in *Selected Works of John Calvin: Tracts and Letters*, ed. Henry Beveridge and Jules Bonnet (1851; reprint, Grand Rapids, Mich.: Baker Book House, 1980), 3:413-490.
[6] Calvin, *Institutes*, trans. Battles, 3.25.1
[7] Heidelberg Catechism, Q & A 52, Schaff, *Creeds of Christendom*, 3:324.
[8] Belgic Confession, Art. 37, Schaff, *Creeds of Christendom*, 3:436.
[9] Heidelberg Catechism, Q & A 42, Schaff, *Creeds of Christendom*, 3:320, 321.

Endnotes

[10] Heidelberg Catechism, Q & A 57, Schaff, *Creeds of Christendom*, 3:325.

[11] Quistorp, *Calvin's Doctrine of the Last Things*, 99.

Contributors

ROBERT DECKER is a professor emeritus of the Theological School of the Protestant Reformed Churches.

RUSSELL DYKSTRA is a professor of theology at the Theological School of the Protestant Reformed Churches.

DAVID J. ENGELSMA is a professor of theology at the Theological School of the Protestant Reformed Churches.

GARRETT ERIKS is a minister in the Protestant Reformed Churches.

BARRY GRITTERS is a professor of theology at the Theological School of the Protestant Reformed Churches.

HERMAN HANKO is a professor emeritus of the Theological School of the Protestant Reformed Churches.

RONALD HANKO is a minister in the Protestant Reformed Churches.

DAVID HIGGS is a minister in the Evangelical Presbyterian Church of Australia.

STEVEN KEY is a minister in the Protestant Reformed Churches.

KENNETH KOOLE is a minister in the Protestant Reformed Churches.

DALE KUIPER is a minister emeritus of the Protestant Reformed Churches.

MARK SHAND is a minister in the Evangelical Presbyterian Church of Australia.

CHARLES TERPSTRA is a member of the Protestant Reformed Churches.

Visit the RFPA website www.rfpa.org

Follow the link to the *Standard Bearer*

View current issue in PDF
or
Standard Bearer archives

The *Standard Bearer* archives are available for viewing, printing and more importantly, are searchable. Type in a key word or phrase and the database will do the searching. The speed of the search has recently been improved. This service makes available a vast amount of doctrinal, historical, and interesting information.

Soon all of the issues will be online.

We invite those interested in subscribing to the
Standard Bearer to phone
the Reformed Free Publishing Association
or visit our website
to request:

a free sample copy
or
10 free issues
or
a first-year subscription at half-price

Call 616-457-5970
Monday, Wednesday–Friday 9:00 A.M.-4 P.M.

Visit www.rfpa.org anytime

Appreciation for the *Standard Bearer*

Covenant Reformed Newsletter, which is mailed to 574 people in the United Kingdom, carried an article that promoted the *Standard Bearer*. It stated the following:

"The *SB* is a magazine that teaches, defends, and applies the Reformed faith, the message of the Bible. It is a well-written, clear, hard-hitting, and refreshingly Reformed magazine in a day of grievous departure from Jesus Christ. First appearing in 1924, it is reputedly the second oldest continuously published Reformed magazine in North America."

"I have in my library, each issue of the *SB* since my first subscription (1979) with few exceptions that I shared with others. It is true that many issues are redundant, but the marvel that I attest to, is that the spirit of my savior God continues to raise up faithful men that have kept the faith once delivered to the saints. The *SB* is an encouragement to be a voice in the wilderness of doctrinal meandering."

—*a reader in Maine*

"Thank you for your biblical base. *Sola scriptura!*"

—*a reader in New Mexico*

"Thank you for your ministry to the saints. I first heard about the RFPA through our home school curriculum. I then came across the *Standard Bearer*. I have greatly appreciated it. The articles consistently lead me to the Word of God and a focus on the Lord Jesus Christ."

—*a reader in New York*

THE VOICE of HISTORIC CHRISTIANITY

Since 1924 the *Standard Bearer* has faithfully and boldly witnessed to the faith of the Protestant Reformation as set forth in the Reformed and Presbyterian creeds.

This semi-monthly, twenty-four-page magazine explains and defends Reformed doctrine (eg., sovereign, particular grace, grounded in eternal election); teaches the Reformed life of the church and believer (eg., Reformed church government and the covenantal life of the Reformed family); and vigorously combats old and new errors that threaten the Reformed faith and life (eg., denial of the infallibility of Holy Scripture; advocacy of a universal love and grace of God; and the charismatic movement, root and branch).

In an age of confusion and compromise, the *Standard Bearer* is a trumpet giving a clear and certain sound (Ezek. 33; 1 Cor. 14:8). Unashamed of the gospel of salvation by grace alone and of the law that regulates the life of holiness, the *Standard Bearer* not only calls Protestant saints to the great battles of our time but also explores and develops the riches of the Reformed faith.

Published by the Reformed Free Publishing Association, the *Standard Bearer* is now one of the oldest continuously published religious periodicals in the United States and is mailed throughout the world.

Reformed Free Publishing Association
1894 Georgetown Center Drive, Jenison, Michigan 49428-7137
Ph: 616-457-5970 Fax: 616-457-5980 www.rfpa.org